THE EFFECTIVE INTERPRETING SERIES

English Skills Development

Teacher's Guide

Carol J. Patrie

Attention: Schools and Distributors

Quantity discounts for schools and bookstores are available.

For information, please contact:

DawnSignPress
6130 Nancy Ridge Drive
San Diego, CA 92121
858-625-0600 V/TTY 858-625-2336 FAX
ORDER TOLL FREE 1-800-549-5350
VISIT US AT www.dawnsign.com

The Rosetta Stone

The Rosetta Stone appears throughout the series as a symbol of translation's importance to mankind. The basalt slab was discovered in July 1799 in the small Egyptian village of Rosette on the western delta of the Nile. The stone's inscription in hieroglyphic, demotic, and Greek languages led to a crucial breakthrough in research regarding Egyptian hieroglyphs. This key to "translating silent images" into a living language symbolizes the importance of accurate transmissions of messages from one language into another.

The Rosetta Stone now resides in the British Museum in London.

Contents

Acknowledgments

This book is the result of the dedicated involvement of many people. Each of them has shaped part of my overall vision for this work and the series of which it is a part. The vision I hold is that this work will assist interpreters, interpreters in training, and their teachers as they work to improve their skills in interpretation, and in so doing will enhance the field of interpretation as a whole. I believe that divine providence led me to DawnSignPress and Joe Dannis. Joe is the *sine qua non* of this work. Without Joe's generous support this work would never have reached fruition. Joe has unwaveringly believed in me and my vision from the very start. Such unconditional support is most rare and deeply appreciated. I thank Becky Ryan for sharing her wonderful literary gifts and talents with me. Her analysis of my work and insightful feedback made this work better than I imagined it could be. She has been a steady source of encouragement and strength in all phases of this project, many above and beyond the call of duty. Joseph Josselyn's skill and precision in video editing have played an important role in creating this exciting instructional package. I thank Earl Fleetwood for his detailed and valuable feedback on the content of this book and for his suggestions for improvement. I deeply appreciate Melanie Metzger's insightful review of the manuscript and video. I am honored to have her as a colleague. I am grateful to Phil Carmona and Yoon Lee for their work on the video. I thank each of these people for the gifts they have shared in order to help this book reach you.

Dedication

To my children Renée and Kurt, who are my
unparalled teachers on the Wheel of Time.

Preface

When I became a professional interpreter in 1968, interpreter education for sign language and spoken language interpreters was either rare or nonexistent. Since that time, interpreter education has made great strides. I am pleased to share with you my 32 years of experience as an interpreter and 16 years of experience as an interpreter educator. I am one of the developers of the Master of Arts in Interpretation at Gallaudet University, where I have been teaching interpretation since 1984. The ideas and exercises presented in this book are the result of my work developing materials that practicing and future interpreters can use in or out of the classroom while they study interpretation.

In my experience I have found that one of the greatest problems in interpreter education is a lack of materials for use in the classroom. An even more severe problem is the lack of study materials that practicing and future interpreters can use on their own, either for refresher practice or for continuing professional development. Interpretation is a very complex skill that requires hours of appropriate practice and too often interpreters do not have access to practice materials that lead to improvement. Skills within a language, that is intralingual skills, must be fully developed before one can begin learning to transfer a message from one language to another. Intralingual skills development is also called preinterpreting skills development. It is my hope that given the materials for developing intralingual skills in English provided herein, practicing and future interpreters will find preinterpreting skills development to be rewarding and effective.

Successful interpreters rely on many intralingual skills, or skills within one language, in their everyday work. The development of these skills is not intuitive or automatic. Most intralingual skills needed during the interpretation process must be developed through a careful sequence of learning activities. Isolating specific intralingual skills and learning them one at a time is the best approach to learning complex new skills; learning new skills one at a time allows mastery of individual skills and a feeling of success. However, control over the intralingual components of the interpretation process is necessary but not sufficient for success in simultaneous interpreting, as intralingual skills are generally not used in isolation and must be synthesized in the process of simultaneous interpretation.

The interpretation process comprises component skills that are interactive and interdependent. An interpretation can only be as successful as the weakest aspect of the process. Mastery of the main components of the interpretation process should begin with strengthening skills in one's first language (L1), in this case, English. The materials within this book provide an innovative and exciting way to develop intralingual skills in English that form the basis for good interpretation skills. I challenge you as a teacher of interpretation to convey the importance of these materials to your students.

Description of the Materials

This set of materials includes a teacher's guide, a student workbook, and a videotext. The teacher's guide includes all of the information in the student workbook plus instructions for the teacher. Both the student and the teacher's books refer to the exercises on the videotext. In the upper right corner of the videotext you will see the unit and exercise number displayed. For example, Ex. 1.2 refers to the second exercise in Unit 1. These materials cover the following topics: the relationships between form and meaning, lexical substitution, paraphrasing propositions, paraphrasing discourse, main idea identification, and summarizing.

Introduction to the Teacher's Guide for English Skills Development

Why This Approach?

One of the reasons that the study of the interpretation process is so challenging is that the nature of the interpretation process itself has resisted definition and description. Without descriptors of the interpretation process, it has been difficult for teachers of interpretation to effect predictable change in student performance as a result of contact with interpreter education curricula. There are a number of models of the interpretation process. No two are exactly alike, but all models suggest that interpretation is a multistage process (Moser, 1997). Gonzalez *et al.* (1991, p. 335) propose the Simultaneous Human Information Processing Model (SHIP). This model is quite different from other models because it is three-dimensional and portrayed in a circular rather than linear fashion and incorporates principles of more linear models into a more powerful model. (Please see Gonzalez *et al.*, 1991, for a more complete description.) Another point that Moser makes is that although most researchers will agree that interpretation is a multistage process, they do not agree on the names of the stages or the contents of the stages. In her conclusion, Moser states that "A powerful model of the interpreting process must be broad enough to include aspects that reflect the complex, time constrained multitasking environment of simultaneous interpreting that involves a high degree of cognitive processing" (Moser, 1997, p. 194). For detailed information on the models mentioned, please refer to the chapter by Moser in Danks *et al.* (1997).

The student workbook was developed along the lines of Gile's (1995) Effort Model because it provides a clear and simple framework for the importance of cognitive processing tasks. Gile's model suggests that in the process of learning interpretation, certain tasks are better presented before others. Moreover, there is limited capacity for specific aspects of the interpretation process, but this capacity must be greater than what the interpretation process requires. By mastering intralingual skills, students gain assurance and increase linguistic capacity.

Basic Assumptions about Interpreter Education

There are several assumptions about interpreter education that form the basis of this text. These assumptions are based on the work of many interpreter educators who have published their work via CIT, American Translators Association, or the John Benjamin's Translation Library. I am strongly in favor of these assumptions and I used them as the basis for my work in teaching interpretation in the past 16 years. The first assumption is that tasks that are relatively less cognitively demanding should appear in the curriculum and be mastered prior to tasks that are more demanding. For example, cognitive tasks such as immediate and delayed repetition and pattern inference are thought to be easier or more manageable for new interpreting students than more demanding tasks such as consecutive or simultaneous interpreting. (A discussion of these terms is provided in the workbook.) The second assumption is that mastery of tasks at a certain level indicates readiness to move on to a more difficult level. The third assumption is that training should proceed from intralingual exercises, which may be taught concurrently with cognitive exercises, to interlingual exercises. The fourth assumption is that consecutive interpreting should follow translation, which in turn should be followed by simultaneous interpreting of monologues, and then dialogues.

A fifth assumption is that interpreters must have a high level of intralingual proficiency. Drills and skills in English are often overlooked or neglected in interpreter education programs. This may be due to the enormous amount of material that must be covered in the interpreter education curriculum, leaving little time for English skills. However, it is essential that interpreter educators take a strong stand on developing English skills in potential interpreters before attempting to develop the other skills needed to become an interpreter. When interpreter educators insist on well-developed, well-controlled English skills, students will also realize the importance of high levels of English proficiency.

The sixth assumption is that in addition to above-average English proficiency skills, interpreters must have high-level cognitive manipulation skills. Intralingual skills and cognitive manipulation skills underlie the more complex skill of simultaneous interpreting. The development of these skills can reduce the amount of effortful processing that is needed to perform these component skills. Lessons and educational experiences that are logically sequenced can lead to more effective learning and teaching experiences. A logical sequence could begin with designing a curriculum, the courses in it, and the lessons within the courses, and then teaching the individual lessons. Next the teacher needs to evaluate the success of the lessons by examining both student and teacher outcomes. The next logical step is to provide feedback to students that will allow them to improve their outcomes. Then the teacher can plan the subsequent lesson. This teacher's guide is designed to help you follow a logical sequence in teaching and evaluating English skills as they relate to development of the interpreting process.

These assumptions regarding the appropriate sequencing of experiences in interpreter education and the importance of strong skills in one's first language underlie all of the information and exercises that follow. Effective interpreter training can lead to enhanced job satisfaction. Greater job satisfaction for individuals can lead to improved levels of professionalism. Improved levels of professionalism among interpreters can ultimately lead to greater consumer satisfaction.

How to Use the Teacher's Guide

This teacher's guide consists of the workbook plus directions and ideas for the teacher. Information intended for the teacher is presented in *italics* in each unit. The italicized information includes teaching ideas as well as possible answers to the exercises. Teachers are encouraged to expand on the instructional ideas presented here. Write your own teaching ideas in the margins and spaces provided. Careful planning of meaningful exercises can make instructional time more valuable for teachers and students. Please read *How to Use This Book* to be sure you and your students have the same understanding about using the book. Ideally, you will read the entire student text and review the video before using either with your students to allow you to be fully aware of the content of the book and video.

Each unit has an introduction section and a section that explains the relevance of that concept to the interpretation process. In each unit there are discussion questions designed to familiarize students with the concepts before beginning the exercises. The exercises have directions for you in *italics* and directions for the students. The directions to the teacher appear only in the first exercise in each unit, but should be followed for each exercise in that unit. The tape is closed-captioned. The captions should not be displayed during the exercise when hearing students are practicing with the material. The length of time of each video selection is included in the directions. You may want to do a dry run with the videotape and exercises to determine how many exercises can be done during class time and how many can be assigned for homework. Some exercises can be done in group format and others require individual recordings by students and are best done individually. There are study questions for each exercise on the videotape. Each spoken English selection on the videotape has been transcribed, and each line of the transcript is numbered to make class discussions easier. A five-step follow-up is an integral part of each exercise. The five-step process is explained below. A progress tracking sheet included at the end of each unit allows students to have a consistent place to record the dates of their work and questions related to the work. The tracking sheet also allows you to monitor student progress easily.

The five-step follow-up is summarized here and explained in detail beginning on page 36.

Step 1   Observation

This allows an objective view of the work just performed by reviewing it as soon as possible after it is completed.

Step 2   Selection

Select the portions of work that are most satisfactory and those that are most troublesome. This step allows students to begin to see which parts of their work are satisfactory and which are not.

Step 3   Analysis

Analyze for accuracy. This step allows students to begin to analyze the areas of their work that need improvement. This important step allows for a shift of responsibility from teacher to student in determining adequacy of work performed.

Step 4   Assessment

Look for underlying reasons for successes or errors. This step often will need teacher input, especially for the novice interpreter. It is very important to determine why errors are occurring, not just that they occur.

Step 5   Action

Develop a plan for action based on analysis and assessment. This step provides students the opportunity to isolate a specific skill and practice it, allowing a feeling of mastery of a specific aspect of the interpretation process. In the case of English skills development it may mean redoing the same exercise in order to get the "feel" of correctly managing the information.

Rating Scales

You may wish to attach a rating scale to each component of the exercises; performance, study questions, and follow-up, when a number or letter grade is needed or desired for an exercise or for a course. For example, in step 1, a five-point scale may be assigned. A sample is presented here. Teachers may vary point assignments to suit their own systems. It is important to decide in advance of conducting an exercise or course how various aspects of the exercise or course will be graded and weighted.

Sample Rating System

5 points = reviewed all portions of the work carefully

4 points = reviewed all portions of the work

3 points = skimmed all portions of the work

2 points = skimmed some of the work

1 point = did not follow instructions

0 points = did not do the work

Teachers may adapt this rating system to meet their own needs. It is customary in most academic settings to present the grading policies in the course syllabus, which should be distributed to student interpreters on the first day of class. This can help students and teachers be clear as to what is expected and when it is due.

Alternatively, you may wish to use a more global and less quantative approach to rating student work. A more complete description of rating options appears on page 20.

Grading Student Work

In general, most colleges and interpreter training programs must award grades to students who are enrolled in courses. Grading student performance is usually one of the most difficult aspects of teaching interpretation. Naturally, we would all prefer to have a completely nonevaluative approach when working with students. However, sometimes student interpreters do not perform at levels that will predict success later in the curriculum and possibly in the profession. Teachers of interpretation have an obligation to the profession to provide student interpreters accurate and meaningful feedback experiences that are supportive, encouraging, and informative. At the same time, teachers want student interpreters to develop accuracy and autonomy in monitoring their own work. This text provides approaches for tracking student progress and encouraging the development of independent and accurate self-monitoring skills by asking students to take responsibility for their work immediately. Accountability for one's work is accomplished via the study questions and the five-step follow-up for each major exercise.

As stated previously, it is important to decide in advance of teaching the course which exercises will be graded, how they will be graded, and how individual exercise grades affect the overall grade. The time taken to generate a reasoned approach to tracking student progress will ultimately save time for both student interpreters and teachers. Ideally, similar grading polices used in each program's curriculum would result in time savings and lead to a more satisfying semester or quarter for all involved.

Teachers must also decide if grades will be based on proficiency, improvement, or some combination of both. Is it appropriate to reward students for doing something well if they already have some expertise in that skill? Teachers are faced with this kind of question when experienced interpreters are enrolled in classes with less experienced students. Naturally, grading policies must be consistent and uniform for all students enrolled in a course. Some teachers prefer to grade for improvement in the earlier parts of the course and proficiency at the end of the course. This could be handled by a combination of exercise grades, based on improvement that might equal 50% of the overall grade, and synthesis grades. Synthesis grades could be determined by end-of-course proficiency exams in which student interpreters demonstrate that they are able to combine the component skills of the course. This latter approach is generally referred to as proficiency testing. Some teachers may want to use the five-point rating system on student answers to the study questions and the follow-up questions or some combination of both, depending on the goals set at the beginning of the course.

Best results are achieved when exercises are presented in the context of a course and the course is presented in the context of a curriculum. Content of individual courses should be developed with the overall goals of the curriculum in mind. The outcomes of each course should lead to the beginning point of the course that follows. All courses in the curriculum should lead to the mastery of curricular goals.

Feedback to Students

Whenever people are learning a new skill they can benefit from guidance from a person who has more experience, such as a teacher or mentor. That guidance is generally difficult to provide in a meaningful way in interpreter education classes if the class size is over ten. The Conference of Interpreter Trainers has published a position paper that states that the ideal class size for interpreter education is six to ten students (1998). Unfortunately, in many programs, the class size is indeed greater than ten. With that current reality in mind, this text has been created to have the students take responsibility for their work at certain levels of review and analysis. However, even if the process is streamlined, the importance of the role of direct input from teacher to student with meaningful guidance for improvement cannot be overemphasized. A few suggestions are provided here to assist teachers with the important process of providing meaningful guidance to students.

Teachers should remember to comment directly on the work and not on the student. Commenting on the work will, in turn, encourage students to do the same. This objectivity will be useful to students, as they eventually become peer supports for each other as classmates and later as professional colleagues. As a result of having clearly planned exercises at hand, teachers can focus more closely on student performance goals. This will lead to more immediate and meaningful feedback.

It is essential for teachers to provide accurate and meaningful feedback as early in the interpreter education program as possible. Every interpreter educator has witnessed a student who clearly had minimal aptitude and ability for interpretation nonetheless graduate because the program and the courses in it had no means of weeding out students who were not progressing satisfactorily. This teacher's guide, student workbook, and video provide assistance in quantifying student performances in a meaningful way.

Teachers can also help students develop insight into the processes used in the exercises. Even if a student says "I don't know how or why that is my answer" the teacher can help students realize how they arrived at that decision. Since it is crucial to develop insight into the process of interpretation, the teacher can use his or her own processes and make them explicit to help students see the many components and decisions that are a part of the interpretation process. Further information regarding teaching interpretation is available in some of the citations listed at the end of this work.

Equipment and Language Laboratory Ideas

The process of learning to interpret requires the use of specific audiovisual equipment. I first describe the ideal situation and then the minimum requirements. Programs are encouraged to obtain the best possible equipment in sufficient quantities so that the instructional contact time during the interpreter education program is maximized.

The ideal situation is a language lab with a carrel for each student or possibly one carrel for two students. In each carrel there should be a video camera that records the student output onto a local VCR in that same carrel. There should be a second VCR for playback of videos and a TV monitor with good resolution. The recording device should allow the student to record source language and target language simultaneously onto a single videotape. Each carrel should have a headphone that allows the student to hear either the source or the target language. The headset may have a microphone built in or there may be a separate microphone to record the student's voice. A high-quality audiocassette recorder should be an integral part of each carrel. An intercom system should allow the student and teacher to interact via voice or sign without interfering with other students.

The ideal teacher's console should allow the teacher to group students or allow each student to work independently. The teacher's console should allow the teacher to broadcast a source tape to some or all students. An intercom system should allow the teacher to call on an individual student without disturbing other students or to speak to the entire class at once through the system. The console should also allow the teacher to listen and watch each student work without interruption. It should also be possible for the teacher to record samples of student work at the teacher console. Such a system is in operation at Gallaudet University.

At minimum the program should provide a VCR and TV monitor for each student as well as one video camera for every one or two students. This arrangement does not allow source and target to be recorded simultaneously but it does allow students to record their own work during class time. It does not allow the teacher to interact privately with each student.

In either the ideal lab or the minimal lab, adequate space is required for the equipment so students can work without interfering with each other. In situations where the program cannot provide adequate space and equipment for interpreter education, then students in those programs will be required to own equipment or have access to equipment. Specifically each student will need access to a VCR, TV, videocamera, and audio recorder. These equipment requirements should be made clear to prospective students before they enter the program.

The approach to interpreter education used here is a highly interactive one that is based on research and theory, but is reliant on frequent and meaningful interaction between students and their teachers. The approaches to analysis, feedback, and the sample rating system are suggested as guidelines. Feel free to incorporate these or modify them to suit your teaching style. You can assign some or all of the exercises, study questions, and follow-up according to the time available and student needs. Within each unit exercises are arranged from easiest to more difficult. If you choose to omit some of the exercises, those exercises could be used for at-home study or extra credit. Assigning all exercises, all study questions, and all follow-up provides the strongest impact on student performance.

The student workbook starts here. Directions to the teacher are interwoven in italics in the workbook.

Introduction to English Skills Development

The Importance of English Language Skills

This workbook focuses on the development of skills within English. Many authors have written about the importance of language competence in interpreter and translator education. When skills are developed *within* a language, these skills are called *intralingual*. When the skills are mastered and effectively used, language competence is achieved. In developing mastery of intralingual skills, it is best to begin in one's first language (L1). The importance of developing and refining skills in L1 is often overlooked in interpreter education. Some may think that being able to read, speak, and understand L1 is enough, and that it is only necessary to study a second language (L2), while overlooking development of first language skills. Roda Roberts writes, "Language competency, which covers the ability to manipulate with ease and accuracy the *two* languages involved in the interpreting process, is a prerequisite for successful interpreting of a message, for the message is mediated through language." (1992, p. 1, emphasis added). She further subdivides the idea of language competency by writing that language competency includes the "ability to understand the source language in all its nuances and the ability to express oneself correctly, fluently, clearly and with poise in the target language" (p. 2).

It is clear that intralingual skills must be well developed in both languages used in the interpretation process. When intralingual skills are well developed, the amount of effort needed to process information is less. Since simultaneous interpreting is a very difficult task, it is best to reduce the amount of effort needed by mastering the component skills before combining them into the more cognitively complex skills needed for simultaneous interpretation.

Moser-Mercer (1984) suggests that competence in monolingual exercises, or exercises within one language, can be a predictor for success in interpreter training (p. 43). Arjona (1984) writes, "The complexity of the communication process in which a translation or interpretation practitioner must function requires nothing less than superior mastery of the language systems involved. Anything less jeopardizes the standards of performance which of necessity must be professionally assured" (p. 3). Arjona suggests that the goal of interpreter training programs is to allow graduates to function with a "minimum competency, proficiency and mastery level needed to perform successfully in real life situations" (p. 3). She explains that the term "minimum competency" does not mean rock bottom. She uses minimum competency to mean the ability to meet the minimum requirement for mastering the task. She goes on to say that candidates for graduation from an interpreter education program must be able to "routinely translate or interpret the message accurately and appropriately, thus bridging the communication gap in a meaningful manner" (p. 6). This means that each individual graduating from a program must be able to perform well against standards for entry to the profession.

In 1994, I conducted a national survey of project directors of federally funded interpreter training grants. I asked these leaders in the field if there was a "readiness-to-work gap." Another way to look at this question is to ask if program exit standards match up with the requirements of entry to the profession. "In response to the survey, the project directors stated unequivocally that this gap exists. They report that as educators, they observe that at the end of interpreter education programs, few graduates are employment-ready. As employers of interpreters, they report that recent program graduates often do not have the necessary skills to enter the job market" (Patrie, 1994, p. 53).

In order to have reliable interpretation skills upon graduation from a two-year program in interpretation it is essential to have strong language skills in at least two languages *upon entry* to the interpretation program. While some programs may evaluate skills in a second language, it is important to realize that first language skills in English are equally important and must be evaluated before an individual enters an interpretation program and improved upon if necessary. It is generally the case that English skills do need improvement during interpreter education in order to ensure reliable interpretation skills upon program completion. When interpreter education programs attempt to introduce a second language and teach interpretation at the same time, the results are unreliable in terms of mastery of interpretation.

When a new interpreter is well prepared to enter the job market, then it is likely that this interpreter will demonstrate a high level of professionalism. Higher levels of professionalism can lead to greater consumer satisfaction and greater recognition and appreciation of the profession of interpretation overall.

The Goal of This Workbook and Video

The purpose of the workbook and accompanying videotape is to improve and enhance your skills in English so that you will have a strong understanding of English usage before you attempt to interpret from or to English. It is important to develop English skills with conscious effort, even if English is your first language. You may not have had the opportunity before now to study your first language as an adult. If English is your second language, this workbook provides you with specific skills that will build confidence in your English skills. As you use this workbook your English skills improve and your awareness of the importance of these skills improves.

An increased awareness of English usage leads to a more reliable interpretation. A reliable interpretation naturally communicates as much as possible of the original meaning. So, it is important to be sure that the meaning of the original message has been correctly analyzed and understood, as far as conditions permit. The seven units in this workbook are designed to provide practice in intralingual skills in English to help ensure that the original message is correctly understood and analyzed. Strong intralingual skills in English are a stepping stone to professional-level simultaneous interpretation skills.

The simultaneous interpretation process is not actually a linear sequence of skills performed one at a time. The various parts of the simultaneous interpretation process, listening, analyzing, transferring the message into another language, and finding expression for that idea, all interact with each other as the speaker continues speaking and the interpreter continues interpreting. It can be overwhelming and not very successful to try to master all the parts of the process at once. Instead, it is more effective to learn how to master the component skills in the interpretation process and then synthesize the component skills into the process of simultaneous interpretation.

Just as the overall process of interpretation is not really linear, the component skills are not linear either. During the actual process of interpretation, specific English skills are dynamic and interact with each other and with other processes. English skills do not appear as discrete units in the interpretation process. Seven important English skills are presented in this workbook. These English skills are separated into seven units in this workbook for two reasons. First, ineffective results commonly are achieved when a student attempts to learn the interpretation process as a whole and has no prior experience in interpretation. The second reason for separating the seven skills is the easy identification of a problem area. Separating the component skills allows you to experience mastery of the components of the larger process.

Why English Skills Are Important

In describing essential criteria for acceptance into interpreter education, Moser-Mercer (1983, p. 61) suggests that "superior command of the English language is the most important". She points out that in a two-year interpreter education program, not much time can be devoted to strengthening one's first language. In addition to strong intralingual skills, interpreters must have high-level cognitive manipulation skills. Intralingual skills and cognitive manipulation skills are two of the skills that underlie the more complex skill of simultaneous interpreting. The development of these skills can reduce the amount of effortful processing that is needed to perform these component skills. According to Kohn and Kalina (1996), "Automation of strategic processes also plays an important role, for only if routine decision processes are performed more or less automatically will the interpreter have enough capacity and attention to solve the more intricate and complex linguistic problems."

Gonzalez *et al.* (1991) emphasize the importance of routinization, or making conscious acts become more automatic. "Therefore any skill that once demanded much focused attention may become unconscious over time with practice. Conscious attention to the interpreting task thereafter may actually interfere with performance" (p. 333). As the interpretation process becomes more routinized less effort is needed. "After interpreters acquire the skill, it is difficult for them to describe what is actually happening. Even when interpreters have managed to make many of the processes in interpretation more automatic, interpretation is still a highly demanding and cognitively complex task." The more that the component skills can be routinized, the better for the overall interpretation performance.

The systematic development of the intralingual skills that underlie the interpretation process is very important. If these skills are not developed and available, then there is a much greater chance that the skills which must follow such as translation, consecutive interpretation, and simultaneous interpretation will not be strongly grounded in basic skills. The resulting deficit could lead to interpretations that are skewed or that contain errors. When more advanced skills do not have a firm base, more effortful processing is required during the interpretation process. When more effortful processing is needed the likelihood of fatigue is increased. Increased fatigue leads to a corresponding increase in errors in interpretation.

Quick access to intralingual skills underlies many of the more complicated aspects of the interpretation process. Interpreters must be able to quickly make sense out of what they see and hear, decide what the message means, and decide how to transfer that message into another language with split-second accuracy. Shreve and Koby (1997) point out that during the past 25 years, there has been much interest in describing the processes associated with interpreting. They point out that these mental operations are largely "hidden," yet form a complex and essential part of the interpretation process. One way to look at these hidden aspects of the interpretation process is to study models of interpretation. Models of interpretation are theoretical; they attempt to describe the process of interpretation and how the process might affect the product of the interpretation.

Models of the Interpretation Process

There are a number of models of the interpretation process. No two are exactly alike, but all models suggest that interpretation is a multistage process. Moser (1997) summarizes some of the better known models of interpretation.

She mentions the following models: Gerver (1976), Moser-Mercer (1978), Kitano (1993), Pradis (1994), and a summary of Daro and Fabbro's (1994) model of memory during interpretation. Moser points out that many models use an information processing approach to explain the interpretation process. Information systems models are based on computer-style operations. This kind of analysis will be necessarily somewhat flawed since human minds do not operate exactly as do computers. Another point that Moser makes is that even though most researchers will agree that interpretation is a multistage process, they do not agree on the names of the stages or the contents of the stages. Moser states that "A powerful model of the interpreting process must be broad enough to include aspects that reflect the complex, time constrained multitasking environment of simultaneous interpreting that involves a high degree of cognitive processing" (1997, p. 194). For detailed information on the models mentioned, please refer to the chapter by Moser in Danks (1997).

In this workbook, I emphasize Gile's (1995) Effort Model because it provides a clear and simple framework for the importance of cognitive processing tasks. Gile's Effort Model provides a powerful explanation for the importance of developing intralingual skills before learning the interpretation process. The model shows that processing capacity for interpreting is available in limited supply and is not automatic.

According to Gile (1995), many of the mental operations required in the interpretation process are nonautomatic and require conscious effort. He suggests that there are three main effort areas in the interpretation process. The first is the Listen and Analysis Effort, which deals with comprehension, the Production Effort, which includes speech planning and verbal output, and the Memory Effort, which deals with the stresses placed on the short-term memory system. These three efforts are integrated by the Coordination Effort. Gile also suggests that each interpreter has certain capacities within each of these areas of effort. Ideally, the interpreter has more capacity than is currently required by the interpretation task. This workbook provides clear approaches to developing the intralingual skills that make up the components of the Effort Model.

Regardless of which model of interpretation you choose to study, you will soon see that all models require that the incoming message be analyzed and understood before any part of the transfer process can begin. In order to accomplish an accurate analysis of the incoming English message, it is essential to have strong English intralingual skills.

When to Develop English Skills

If you are a novice or new interpreter, English skills should be developed before moving on to more advanced skills in the interpretation process. If you are beyond the beginning stages of an interpreter education program, or are already a practicing interpreter, you can still benefit from practice in English skills, either as a refresher course or for professional skill maintenance.

The exercises in this book can be used as review and refresher material. Often students in interpreter education programs may experience the "plateau effect" in training. The plateau effect occurs when skills appear to no longer develop as rapidly as they did earlier in the training process. This is a common occurrence. When progress seems to stagnate, it is often useful to go back to an earlier stage of skill development and practice at that level. Taking time to go back and review skills is a positive step because it increases confidence, builds mastery, and often provides the springboard to further progress.

This workbook can also benefit practicing interpreters. Practicing interpreters may not have had the benefit of studying the individual skills that make up the interpretation process. Practicing interpreters often search for specific ways to improve their interpretation skills. Reviewing and practicing the components of the interpretation process, such as intralingual skills, can be meaningful and productive for the experienced interpreter who wishes to work independently on skill improvement. Strong intralingual skills form a good basis for more complex skills in the interpretation process.

Specific English Skills

The English skills in this book are presented in a sequence that ideally occurs early in an interpreter education program, and can also be used for drills at later stages of development. This sequence of skills optimally can be practiced in your first language and then in the second language. Intralingual skills which support the development and maintenance of interpreting skills include understanding the difference between visual form and meaning and between spoken form and meaning; paraphrasing at the lexical level, proposition level, and discourse level; finding the main point; and summarizing. A description of these skills is summarized below. Each of these skills is relevant to any level of experience in interpretation, beginning, intermediate, or advanced.

It is important to have a clear understanding of the terminology used in this book. The main terms for each unit are described here.

Visual Form

The term visual form can refer to a printed picture or visualization. It is a representation of an idea but does not use words to convey the idea. Pictures are used in some of the exercises to help you understand that the picture of an idea is not the same thing as the expression of that idea in spoken English. Although the idea "behind" the picture and the corresponding visualization could be the same, the form is different when an idea is expressed in a picture and when it is expressed in spoken or written English. It is important to realize that form is arbitrary, whether it is a printed word, visualization, or picture. "The fact that external form is arbitrary can be seen in the phenomenon of synonyms. Two words can represent the same underlying concept, like 'car' and 'auto' and single words like 'bear' and 'nut' can represent multiple concepts" (Gonzalez et al., 1991, p. 299).

Form and Meaning

The first two units deal with the important distinctions between form and meaning. The issue of form and meaning is complex. The distinctions between form and meaning are often overlooked, yet these distinctions create the basis for a reliable interpretation.

Form refers to the observable aspects of the language, in this case, spoken English and its words, pronunciation of those words, and the way those words are arranged. In this text, the spoken English of the speakers on the videotape is a form that is transcribed for closer scrutiny. The printed transcriptions create yet another form of the same message, the written form.

The meaning can also be referred to as the message. Seleskovitch and Lederer (1989) state "the sense" or ideas are expressed in a specific form or language. The form of an English word can be spoken or written, but in either case, it is a symbol for the concept or thing to which it refers. For example, the printed word "cat" and the spoken word "cat" are not the cat itself. Both the printed and the spoken versions are symbols that represent the real cat.

Saussure proposed the idea of a "linguistic sign" as a way to describe the link between form and concept: "The linguistic sign unites, not a thing and a name, but a concept and a sound-image." (from Gonzalez *et al.,* 1991, p. 299). Because form and meaning are so closely linked, the distinctions between the two are not obvious to many people. This is one reason that exercises focusing on the distinction between form and meaning are included in this workbook.

Lexical Substitution

Lexical substitution means replacing a word in a specific context with another word that does not change the meaning of the original utterance. Lexical substitution exercises in Unit 3 are designed to improve your vocabulary so that you can quickly replace the original word with another word that does not change the meaning. Topics in Unit 3 include information and practice with the following concepts; words as propositional units, specific and general words, primary and secondary meaning of words, and collocations or the usual arrangement patterns of words.

Paraphrasing Propositions

A proposition is an idea unit. Propositional paraphrasing means restating the message in a different way (form) that does not change the meaning. In Unit 4, exercises in propositional paraphrasing provide practice in restating short utterances in a new form. These exercises provide practice in unpacking or discovering the possible meanings contained in specific utterances.

Paraphrasing Discourse

Discourse paraphrasing means restating a longer text in a different form without changing the meaning. Unit 5 has information and exercises on paraphrasing information at the discourse level and provides opportunities to restate larger amounts of information than occur at the sentence level. At either the sentence or the discourse level, the underlying meaning must not be changed when it is restated.

Main Idea Identification

The main idea in a speech or passage is the central point or most important idea in the speech or passage. Unit 6 provides exercises and information for sorting main ideas from supporting ideas. These exercises allow you to begin to establish the relative importance of various parts of utterances. In the event that some information must be deleted from the interpretation due to the heavy flow of information, it is important to be able to distinguish which aspects are less important. For example, repetitions and paraphrases of information stated earlier by the speaker might be considered of lesser importance than information that occurs only once and is central to the message. Central aspects of the message must not be deleted in the interpretation.

Summarizing

A summary is a brief rendition of the most important points in a passage. A summary can be as short as one sentence, which is sometimes called the gist of the passage, or it could be as long as a paragraph in the case of a longer text. Unit 7 provides exercises in creating concise and accurate summaries to allow you to focus on the most important aspect of the message. In some cases when the information load forces the interpreter to be farther behind the message than is ideal, summarizing can sometimes be used to catch up. Occasionally a consumer may request a summary interpretation. A summary interpretation provides only the main points and is usually provided after the source language has stopped. Summarization skills are important as a developmental tool as well as a professional tool.

Process and Product

In interpreter education there is always much discussion over whether students should focus on the process of interpretation or the product of the interpretation. Both are equally important and should be part of even the earliest stages of training. It is vital that you understand the difference between these two terms and the role they play in your education and training as an interpreter. The process of interpretation is largely invisible. The process is what goes on in your head as you listen, analyze, and transfer the meaning of the message from one language to another. The product, the message rendered in the target language, is the end result of the process.

The processes associated with the interpretation event cannot be recorded or observed by another person. Only via introspection can the interpreter gain insight into their own process and make changes to it. Gile (1995) suggest that adopting a process-oriented approach can optimize training time. In Gile's opinion it is best to focus not just on the end products of the translation process, but rather to include information on "principles, methods and procedures" (p. 10). Gile goes on to support his idea: "By concentrating on the reasons for errors or good choices in Translation rather than on the words or structures produced by the students, teachers devote most of their effective teaching time to Translation strategies and lose little time over their by-products" (p. 11). Gile goes on to say that later in interpreter training programs, additional emphasis must be placed on product, but only after the underlying processes are established.

The product is the observable part of your work. It is the interpretation that the "listener" receives from the "sender" via your interpretation. The product can be recorded for future analysis, while the process cannot. Seal has summarized the results of a recent study of interpreters who wished to improve their skills. In that report, she emphasizes the importance of analyzing one's own work. "Self-analysis, the zenith of any professional development activity, is highly facilitated when we step back and take a look at ourselves. Routine videotaping and observing videotaped performances for strengths and weaknesses and for changes over time is quite possibly the most valuable, yet least frequently accomplished activity we can engage in" (Seal, 1999, p. 14).

How to Use This Book

Information, exercises, and follow-up are provided for each of the seven skill units in this book. The English intralingual skills in this workbook are relationships between visual form and meaning, relationships between spoken English and visual form, lexical substitution, paraphrasing propositions, paraphrasing discourse, main and supporting ideas, and summarizing. These are some of the important components of intralingual skill development. In each unit, a brief introduction provides background information and an explanation of the relevance of that information to the overall interpretation process. The introductory material is followed by a series of exercises specifically designed to apply the concepts and skills presented in the unit. In each unit there are three aspects to each exercise. The first is to respond to the exercise material and record your answers. This allows you to create a product. The second is to answer the study questions. Answering the study questions allows you to examine your product. The third aspect is follow-up. The follow-up allows you to examine the processes used to arrive at the answers (product) that you provided.

All of the exercises (recording, answering the study questions, and completing the follow-up) in each unit may be completed as out of classroom work or as independent work during class time, if appropriate equipment is available. Some of the exercises may also be done in a group format. Units 1, 4, and 7 require individual spoken responses and are best done individually, rather than in a group. Units 2 and 3 can be done in a group setting. Units 5 and 6 have workbook exercises that can be done in a group setting. As this is a workbook, you will read the exercise and respond on paper, without the time pressure of responding to a videotaped exercise. Units 5 and 6 also have real-time exercises that will require spoken responses.

For either independent or group work, this workbook provides complete directions for each exercise. The directions guide you to the correct location on the accompanying videotape. Each exercise has study questions and a follow-up. The study questions help provide focus and insight into your responses to the exercises. The follow-up after each exercise is a form of self-assessment and is fully explained below. The workbook exercises and follow-up provide the opportunity for you to take responsibility for creating work (product) and to analyze and develop strategies for improvement. In this workbook, it is not necessary to translate or interpret any of the English messages. All of the exercises in this workbook are designed to improve and strengthen skills in understanding meaning in English and develop skills in working with English.

What You Need before Beginning the Exercises

You will need specific equipment to get the maximum benefit from these exercises: a VHS VCR with a remote control that will allow pausing and frame advance, a TV monitor, an audio recorder, a blank VHS videotape, a blank audio tape, a quiet place to work, a copy of the video that accompanies this workbook, and this workbook. A video camera enhances the study process but is optional. You will also need three different colored pencils or pens, one each of blue, black, and red.

When and Where You Should Plan to Do the Exercises

Each exercise can be done independently. This means that you should plan to do them either out of class on your own time or in a class format if your training program has a place for you to record your work. Where you do the exercises will depend on your instructor and the equipment available in your interpreter education program. For example, if your program has a language lab that will permit you to work independently and to record your work, then you can do many of the exercises independently while on campus or in class. Exercises in Units 2 and 3 may be done in a group setting without individual recording devices for each student. Your teacher may introduce the exercises to you and go over your results with you. Your teacher may provide similar exercises for you to work on in class, or you may work on some of these exercises in class, depending on your teacher's instructions and lesson plans.

If you are a practicing interpreter and want to work on developing your skills you will still need all of the equipment listed previously and may proceed at your own pace. You may wish to form a study group with other interpreters in order to have a forum to discuss your skill-development work, both product and process.

How Many Times Should You Do the Exercises?

You can benefit from doing each exercise at least twice. This process is called redoing your work. When you do the exercise the first time, the material that you listen to will be "cold," or unfamiliar. The intralingual skills that you are practicing may be new and unfamiliar as well. When you do the exercise the second time, the material will be "warm," or familiar, because you have heard it once. You will be more comfortable with the process the second time. It is a good idea to practice the exercises more than once because this type of practice will allow you to experience good control of the process that you are working on and improve the quality of the process that you use to create the product.

The Five-Step Follow-up

The five-step follow-up is presented after each exercise.
The five parts of the follow-up are:

Step 1	**Observation**
Step 2	**Selection**
Step 3	**Analysis**
Step 4	**Assessment**
Step 5	**Action**

The purpose of the follow-up is to introduce and strengthen the concepts of self-assessment and insight into the process of interpretation. Interpreters who have accurate self-assessment skills can enjoy lifelong learning and continuing education opportunities in a wide variety of settings, even if a teacher or mentor is not available. As Smith (1984, p. 74) wrote, "...we must teach our students to evaluate and to teach themselves. It is the life of a professional." Self-assessment skills lead to accountability in interpretation because they allow you to analyze both the process and the product of your work. Accountability in interpretation means that interpreters can make conscious decisions about both the products and the processes involved in their interpretations and work to see that the interpretations are faithful to the original message. Accountability also means that the interpreter can take responsibility when the interpretation is not faithful to the message and correct the interpretation. A graduate of the Master of Arts in Interpretation at Gallaudet who became very familiar with the follow-up suggests that "The impact of the self assessment available through the follow up process is unparalleled" (Fleetwood, 1998, personal communication).

The five-step follow-up for self-assessment is unprecedented in interpreter education, so you are likely to find it unfamiliar. By developing accurate self-assessment skills, you also develop control over the parts of the interpretation process that should be under the interpreter's control.

In addition to increasing accountability in interpretation, the follow-up for self-assessment allows an objective analysis of either the product or the processes involved in interpretation. This five-step approach to analysis allows for commentary on the work performed rather than on the interpreter who performed it. By carefully doing each part of the follow-up, you will learn the importance of the many component skills of the interpretation process and that each, performed well, is needed for a successful interpretation.

By being able to separate the process into its component skills, you can better understand where to focus your efforts for improvement. Although the interpretation process is not a segmented event in real life, one should study it in smaller, more manageable pieces at first. The follow-up in this book allows you to determine which parts of your work are successful attempts and which parts are less successful. More importantly, it helps you to see which parts of the interpretation process are under your control and which are not.

The five-step follow-up is an exciting way to improve your awareness of your performance. All students want to know "How am I doing so far?" By putting forth the effort to work through the follow-up you will be able to answer this question yourself instead of relying on a teacher to provide all of the feedback on your work. Naturally, if you are just learning the process you will need both your own analysis of your work and your teacher's input.

The follow-up should be started as soon after you complete the exercises as possible. This is important as you may be asked to explain your answers to the study questions and you will be better able to explain your thinking if you do the follow-up immediately after the exercises. Whether you are working individually or in a group the questions and activities in the follow-up could be used in a group discussion format. If you are working in a group format, it is still important to write your answers so you can refer to them later and see the progress you have made in developing self-assessment skills.

A more complete explanation of the follow-up is given on pages 26–28 (Teacher's Guide pages 36–39).

Progress Tracking Sheet

Use this sheet to track your progress with the exercises you have completed. After performing the exercise, answering the study questions, and doing the follow-up, fill in the tracking sheet. Note the date that you completed the exercise and give an indication of your level of accomplishment. You can use either a quantitative or qualitative approach to track your progress.

A quantitative approach uses a point scale. Assigning points to linguistic exercises is arbitrary, but in academic environments you may find the point system more suitable than the qualitative approach. Here is an example of a scale you can use to assign points to your work. Excellent (no serious errors) = 5 points, Good (some errors, but not serious) = 4 points, Fair (many errors, some serious) = 3 points, Not satisfactory = 2 (many errors, most are serious), Poor = 1 point. (Missed the point of the exercise—must redo).

Each performance, each study question, and each follow-up step can be assigned a point value. A zero indicates that the question was not answered and a 5 indicates a full and complete answer. Add the scores in each column (not row) and divide by the number of exercises to get a percentage for first performance, second performance, study questions, and follow-up. It is important to have separate percentages for each of these columns because the scores represent different skills. Remember that a second performance on the same material is considered practice on "warm" or familiar material and should be weighted less than the "cold" or first performance.

A qualitative approach is well suited to those who are studying the material in an independent fashion or those who do not want to attach numbers and percentages to their work. In a qualitative approach you describe your response to your work rather than assigning numbers. Write down enough information to remind yourself of your level of achievement in the performance of the exercises, study questions and follow-up.

The sample chart provides examples of how to note your progress using the quantitative or qualitative approach.

Exercise Number	Date	First Performance	Study Questions	Follow-up Activity	Questions and Reminders	Date	Second Performance
Exercise 1 Quantitative	10/3	35/50 = 70%	20/25 = 80%	20/25 = 80%		11/5	45/50 = 90%
Qualitative		I added information not in the illustration.	Able to see differences in form in most cases. Not sure about meaning.	Analysis area needs work.	Saw a big difference between my answers and those on the tape.		Sentences more accurately depicted the illustrations.
Exercise 2 Quantitative	10/9	40/50 = 80%	20/25 = 80%	25/25 = 100%		11/15	45/50 = 90%
Qualitative		Did not add information, but omitted some detail.	Similarity and difference in meaning is clearer.	Analysis is more accurate.	Can see how different forms can affect meaning.		Added some detail. Better overall.
Exercise 3 Quantitative	10/15	45/50 = 80%	25/25 = 100%	25/25 = 100%		11/21	45/50 = 90%
Qualitative		Accurate in conveying the information, but too wordy.	Pleased with my grasp of material.	Satisfied with my progress in reviewing and analyzing work.	Understanding of material is stronger than my ability in performance.		More concise and accurate.
Quantitative Totals		76%	86%	93%			90%

Visual Form and Meaning

The goal of this unit is to improve awareness of the difference between form and meaning and how this difference becomes crucial in the interpretation process. Read the introductory information in this unit. If you have other information you want to present to your students on the topic of visual form and meaning, prepare that information in an outline to refer to during your lecture. You can make handouts from your outline for students to use. Ask students to discuss the terms visual form and meaning and what they believe these terms mean. Discussion questions are included and should precede the exercises.

Introduction

In this unit, the goal is to emphasize the difference between meaning as conveyed in visual form (illustrations or printed English) and the same idea or meaning expressed in the form of spoken English. This unit introduces the fact that the form of a message can take various shapes while the meaning can remain constant. There are three representations of form found in the exercises in this unit. The three forms are: (1) the visual image, (2) the spoken English created in response to the visual image, and (3) the written transcription of the spoken English. The visual image, the spoken English, and the written English tap the same meaning. The exercises ask you to provide a spoken English utterance in response to a visual image.

Working from a visual image to a spoken form is a particularly effective way to improve intralingual skills because the visual images present concepts and the relationships between objects in the illustrations. Kintsch (1972) explains that concepts can contain meaning and information about relationships that do not rely on a specific language. The visual images in the workbook will allow you to express the names that correspond to the objects shown in the illustrations and the relationships between them without being influenced by the spoken or written forms that express the same idea.

According to Larsen (1984, p. 3) the form of a language consists of its words, phrases, clauses, and sentences that are spoken or written. These forms are also referred to as the surface structure of a language. The meaning is the sense or semantics or deep structure of the message. The issue of form and meaning is central to the study of interpretation, regardless of the languages involved. It is crucial that interpreters know the difference between form and meaning and how this difference can affect the interpretation.

Form

The form of the message is the observable part of the language. In English it is the spoken, graphic, or written form of English and includes information at the word level (vocabulary), phrase, sentence, and discourse level. The order of words at the sentence or phrase level is called syntax. The form is the part of language that can be seen or heard.

Meaning

The meaning is the nonobservable part of communication. The sense, intent, and message are clothed in a form. The meaning is the central kernel or idea that must be clearly understood and conveyed by the interpreter.

Visual Image

The visual images used in this book are simple line drawings that convey meaning without written or spoken language. Relationships between persons or persons and objects are shown in these simple illustrations. No two speakers will respond in exactly the same way to these illustrations. These differences in expression emphasize that a message can be conveyed in several forms without changing the meaning of the message. Each person has a different set of life and linguistic experiences and level of language competence. These differences in experience and language competence will affect the way people see and respond to the illustrations.

The Role of Distinguishing Form from Meaning in the Interpretation Process

Interpreters must be able to convey the meaning from the source language (SL), the language they are working from, into the target language (TL), the language they are working into, without distorting the message. If interpreters follow the form of the source language when they render the message in the target language, there is a high probability that the interpretation will not accurately convey the intended message. An example of this problem can be seen when an interpreter follows the word order of the source language when interpreting into a target language that has a different set of rules for word order. When interpreters follow the form of the source language and disregard the meaning, the result can be a word-for-word transcoding process. The word-for-word approach rarely conveys the intended meaning accurately. Instead, the result is often "word salad." The words presented in the target language may look or seem fine in proximity to each other, just as the components in a salad do, but lack meaningful linguistic relationships to each other. The ideal situation in interpretation is one in which the interpreter has grasped the speaker's intended meaning to the extent that the interpreter's language skill, interpretation skill, and prior knowledge will allow. Then, regardless of the form of the source language, the message is rendered in a syntax and vocabulary that is appropriate to the target language. The better the interpreter understands the meaning the better chance he or she will have to render the message into a form that is appropriate to the form of the target language.

The issue of the difference between form and meaning is further complicated by the fact that often one word or form can have many meanings in a specific language. For example, the word "run" has many meanings but only one form. On the other hand, a single meaning or concept in the source language may have many different words to express it in the target language. For example, the American Sign Language (ASL) sign that is glossed as "SILLY" will require one or more English words to convey its meaning, depending on the its context.

Interpreters must be able to determine the intended meaning of the message in the source language and which form in the target language most appropriately expresses the intended meaning. This decision will ultimately be based on many factors. Some of these factors can include the context of the message, the participants, the cultural aspects of the languages and situation, and the interpreter's level of language ability in both the source and target languages. These factors make it necessary to be able to make quick linguistic decisions during the interpretation process. Structured practice and experience can improve the interpreter's linguistic decision-making.

Discussion Questions

Discuss the following questions with your students to promote insight and increase awareness of the importance of understanding the difference between form and meaning expressed in spoken English.

1. *How does an understanding of the difference between form and spoken English relate to the interpretation process?*

    This is an important question because some students may feel that if English is their first language, they do not need to study English during their interpretation studies. However, most students have not had the opportunity to study English as adults and most have not had the opportunity to discuss the difference between form and meaning. Interpreters need to be aware that many different forms of spoken English could represent a single visual image. This awareness can provide the interpreter with greater linguistic flexibility.

2. *Do you feel you understand a visual image the same way everyone else does?*

    Most students will answer "yes" to this question. This question does not seek to see if the interpreter is an objective observer. Hopefully the interpreter is objective. This question encourages the student to see that each person who views a simple illustration may see it differently from anyone else. The belief that everyone sees things the same way leads users of the same language to believe that they are communicating clearly and understand each other well. In fact, even between two people conversing in the same language, there is usually some loss of intended meaning.

3. *What happens when two people see the same visual image differently?*

    First of all, the two viewers are not likely to realize that they do not see the same things in the visual image. If one or both viewers can realize that there are various ways to see an image, then there is less likelihood that misunderstandings will arise between the two people. If the misunderstanding occurs between friends, a conflict may arise. If the misunderstanding occurs between people who are not of equal status in the context of that conversation, usually the person of lower status will be disadvantaged by the misunderstanding. As students develop increasing awareness of how often people misunderstand each other, it is likely that they will be tempted to explain meanings and misunderstandings to people who are conversing in the same language. Should they? This could become an interesting discussion of the interpreter's role, which generally does not include clearing up misunderstandings between speakers of the same language.

    Naturally, each person will have a different "form" or way of expressing what he or she sees in the illustration. Through these expressions of form, we can determine if we see approximately the same things in a visual image or not.

4. *What will happen if the interpreter does not understand the message conveyed in the visual image but thinks they do understand?*

This is a common situation. When the interpreter misunderstands then the interpretation will be skewed or inaccurate, whether the interpreter is aware of the misunderstanding or not.

5. *What happens when the interpreter does not understand the message conveyed in the visual image and knows that they do not understand?*

This lack of understanding should become apparent very quickly. The interpreter or student will not be able to give linguistic form to the visual image. The interpreter will be at a loss for words.

Visual Form and Meaning Exercises

In this section, the goal is to emphasize the difference between form and meaning using the visual images presented in the workbook. In the accompanying video, two native speakers of English, Diana and Leslie, convey in spoken English what the visual representations mean to them. Their instructions were to look at the entire set of illustrations on the page and create an utterance or sentence that conveys the meaning of each illustration on the page. You will create your own responses to the same visual images. As you compare your spoken English to that of Diana and Leslie, it will become clear that the meaning of the illustrations can and will be expressed in slightly different forms, depending on the way a person chooses to speak English. Even though you and the two speakers are all looking at the same illustrations, it is unlikely that any two sentences for a specific illustration will be exactly the same. So even though the forms are different, the meaning can remain constant. It is also true that variations in expression (form) can slightly alter the meaning. Comparing meanings of the speakers' sentences with each other and with your sentences will help you understand how differences in form can change the meaning of the sentence.

Even though the two speakers have much in common, such as gender, approximate age range, and educational level, you will see that the spoken English forms chosen to express the meanings they understood are quite different. Neither speaker rehearsed their responses in advance of the videotaping. This allowed for a more spontaneous rendition of the meaning as each person understood it. Please note that neither version is considered "right"; rather, each represents the speakers' view and manner of expression. When working from a visual to a spoken form, you will notice that sometimes details can be left out or added. For example, the name of the sort of vehicle into which the woman is loading her wood in the third scenario is mentioned by one speaker but not by another. Sometimes, details are added that cannot be determined from the illustrations. For example, in response to the third scenario, one speaker says the woman is drawing up plans for something special. You will consider whether these omissions or additions substantially changes the meaning of the utterance.

In the following exercises, it is preferable to respond in spoken English. If for some reason you are unable to tape-record or videorecord your spoken English for later analysis, you may write your answer. There are important differences between spontaneously spoken English and written English. Most people do not speak the way they write and vice versa. To make a direct comparison with the responses of the two speakers, it is best to record your spoken responses and then transcribe your spoken English. Compare the transcription of your work with the transcriptions of Diana and Leslie's spoken English. These short scenarios do not contain contextual or cultural information. Additional context can be added for variety in these exercises.

Diana Gorman

Leslie Rach

In the video, the first thing you will see in Unit 1 is Diana and Leslie introducing themselves.

The exercises in Unit 1 are designed to introduce the concepts related to distinguishing form from meaning. Decide if you want to conduct these exercises in class, or if you want the students to do the exercises on their own time. In either case, students must record their responses.

If you decide to do the exercises in class, each student must be able to record their answers on a video or audio recorder. Read the directions and explain them to the students. Allow time for questions after you have given the directions. You should plan at least five minutes to prepare the students for each exercise. Five minutes should be enough, if you have the group's attention, and if all equipment is ready and in working order. Any tapes needed for these exercises must be cued to the correct spot. This includes any tapes that will be used for recording.

In each exercise in Unit 1 comments for the teacher are in italics. The general notes to the teacher appear in Exercise 1.1. Additional comments for other exercises in this unit are included only if necessary.

EXERCISE 1.1

Gardening

Directions

Student Workbook
page 19

This selection is approximately three minutes long. Look at the illustrations and record your responses, listen to the speaker's responses, and then answer the study questions and do the follow-up exercise. You need three different colored pens or pencils for this exercise, red, blue, and black. You will use these to mark on the transcripts of Diana's, Leslie's, and your own responses. Use copy 1 of the transcripts to compare your answers to Diana's and Leslie's answers. Use copy 2 of the transcripts to compare Diana's and Leslie's responses to each other. Each response is numbered. For example, Diana's first response is Diana 1 and Leslie's first response is Leslie 1. Number your responses in the same way using your own name or initials. Use a circle to indicate differences in form. Underline to show differences in meaning.

Record and Transcribe Your Answers

Look at all nine illustrations for exercise 1.1. Record one complete sentence in spoken English on your tape recorder for each of the nine illustrations. Your sentence should include only the information that you obtain by looking at the illustration and that expresses your understanding of the illustration. Remain aware of the context in which the illustration is situated. You should not add or subtract information. Pause after each sentence and think about the information you wish to include in the next sentence.

Transcribe exactly what you recorded on your tape. This will allow you to make a direct comparison of your spoken English with the spoken English of the two speakers. Write the transcript of your responses here.

____

____

____

____

____

____

____

____

____

____

____

____

____

____

Listen to the Spoken Responses of Diana and Leslie on the Video

This is important because we are focusing on using spoken English. The written transcripts are provided as a way to allow analysis of the utterances. Point out to students that written English is different in form than spoken English and that the transcripts are representations of spoken English.

Transcript Copy 1 for *Planting a Garden*

Diana's responses to the illustrations for planting a garden:

Diana 1   A woman is digging in her garden.

Diana 2   She gets out some fertilizer and spreads it throughout the garden.

Diana 3   She then plants some seeds.

Diana 4   She puts wooden stakes throughout the garden.

Diana 5   She then waters the garden.

Diana 6   Then she has to pull weeds out of the garden.

Diana 7   When her tomatoes and other vegetables are ready, she picks them from the garden.

Diana 8   She then slices up all of her vegetables.

Diana 9   Then a woman enjoys a salad made from the vegetables in her garden.

Leslie's responses to the illustrations for planting a garden:

Leslie 1   There is a woman working on her garden, tilling up the soil.

Leslie 2   Now we see her putting down some fertilizer.

Leslie 3   Next she is on her hands and knees putting some seeds into the rows that she's dug up.

Leslie 4   Now she is working with stakes, putting them into the ground and patting the dirt around them.

Leslie 5   Next we see her adding water with a hose, in a fine spray.

Leslie 6   Now we see the woman again on her hands and knees in the garden, pulling out weeds.

Leslie 7   Next we see her picking tomatoes.

Leslie 8   Now she is in the kitchen cutting up her fresh vegetables from

her garden.

Leslie 9   Finally she sits down to enjoy a salad, made of the fruits of

her labor.

Study Questions

Use red to compare your answers to Diana's. Use blue to compare your answers to Leslie's. Use black to compare Diana's and Leslie's responses to each other.

1. With regard to form, do your sentences differ from Diana's? On copy 1, circle any parts of Diana's response that differ in form from yours in red. Circle the corresponding difference in your response in red. For example, if your sentence says "A lady is digging in her garden" and Diana's response is "A woman is digging in her garden" circle the word "lady" in red in your transcript and the word "woman" in red in Diana's transcript.

   You should expect that each student will have some portion of their response circled in red. It is very unlikely that any two responses will be identical in form. Differences in form can be due to added information, omitted information, or misunderstood information.

2. With regard to form, do your sentences differ from Leslie's? On copy 1, circle any parts of Leslie's responses that differ in form from yours in blue. Circle the corresponding difference in your transcript in blue. For example, if your response is "There is a woman working in her garden, digging up the soil" and Leslie's response is "There is a woman working in her garden, tilling up the soil" you would circle the word "digging" in blue on your transcript. Circle the word "tilling" in blue Leslie's response.

   You should expect that each student will have some portion of their response circled in blue. It is very unlikely that any two responses will be identical in form.

3. With regard to meaning, do your sentences differ from Diana's? On copy 1, underline in red any parts of Diana's responses that differ from yours in meaning. Underline the corresponding section of your response in red. For example, if Diana's response Diana 1 is "A woman is digging in her garden" and your response is "A woman is digging in the backyard," you would underline in red the word "garden" in Diana's response and the word "backyard" in your response because the meaning of these two words is different. In this case you should find that the words "garden" and "backyard" already have circles around them to indicate that they do

not share the same form. Because the meaning of these words is different they should also be underlined.

You can expect that the parts of the responses circled in question 1 could also be underlined in response to this question. However, if the circled words are synonyms then the meaning will be approximately the same and not underlined.

4. With regard to meaning, do your sentences differ from Leslie's? On copy 1, underline any of Leslie's responses that differ from yours in meaning in blue. Underline the corresponding response from your transcript in blue. For example, Leslie' response Leslie 1 is "A woman is working in her garden, tilling up the soil." If your response is "A woman is working in her garden, tilling up the compost" you would underline in blue the word "soil" in Leslie's transcript and the word "compost" in yours. In this case, you should find that the word "soil" and the word "compost" are already circled because they do not share the same form. Because the meaning of these words is different they should also be underlined.

You can expect that the parts of the responses circled in question 2 could also be underlined in response to this question. However, if the circled words are synonyms then the meaning is approximately the same and should not be underlined.

5. Using copy 2 of the transcript of Diana's and Leslie's responses, printed below, compare Diana's and Leslie's responses to each other with regard to form. Circle in black any words in Diana's responses that differ in form from Leslie's responses. Do the differences in form create differences in meaning? Write "yes" or "no" for each utterance in the space provided following copy 2.

These comparisons should generate some lively discussions as to whether the responses are equivalent. Some suggested ways of looking at the comparisons follow copy 2.1.

Transcript Copy 2 for *Planting a Garden*

Diana's and Leslie's responses to the illustrations for planting a garden:

Diana I   A woman is digging in her garden.

Leslie I   There is a woman working on her garden, tilling up the soil.

1. Yes. The differences in form affect the meaning. "Tilling and "digging" have

different meanings.

Diana 2   She gets out some fertilizer and spreads it throughout the garden.

Leslie 2   Now we see her putting down some fertilizer.

2. Yes. The differences in form affect the meaning. "Putting down" and "spreading" have different meanings.

Diana 3   She then plants some seeds.

Leslie 3   Next she is on her hands and knees putting some seeds into the rows that she's dug up.

3. Yes. The additional information in Leslie's response changes the meaning.

Diana 4   She puts wooden stakes throughout the garden.

Leslie 4   Now she is working with stakes, putting them into the ground and patting the dirt around them.

4. Yes. The additional information in Leslie's response changes the meaning.

Diana 5   She then waters the garden.

Leslie 5   Next we see her adding water with a hose, in a fine spray.

5. Yes. The additional information in Leslie's response changes the meaning.

Diana 6   Then she has to pull weeds out of the garden.

Leslie 6   Now we see the woman again on her hands and knees in the garden, pulling out weeds.

6. Yes. The additional information in Leslie's response changes the meaning slightly.

Diana 7   When her tomatoes and other vegetables are ready, she picks them from the garden.

Leslie 7   Next we see her picking tomatoes

7. Yes. The additional information in Diana's response changes the meaning.

Diana 8   She then slices up all of her vegetables.

Leslie 8   Now she is in the kitchen cutting up her fresh vegetables from the garden.

8. Yes. The additional information in Leslie's response changes the meaning.

Diana 9   Then the woman enjoys a salad made from the vegetables in her garden.

Leslie 9   Finally she sits down to enjoy a salad, made of the fruits of her labor.

9. No. The differences in form do not affect the meaning. "Fruits of her labor" is

a figurative expression for "vegetables in her garden."

Sample Follow-up—Pat's Answers

The answers of a hypothetical student named Pat are shown here and discussed to help you get started on your own five-step follow-up. Notice the kinds of things included. As you analyze your own work, you can think of it as a mystery. What was missing? What was good? What accounts for your success in the exercises? Why did you miss some aspects? The sooner you can adopt an analytical view of your own work, the sooner your progress in interpretation skills can become reliable. Your answers will be either written in this book or recorded on tape for you to review. For example, when Pat has completed Exercise 1 Visual Images with Meaning Conveyed in Spoken English, s/he will refer to the answers to the study questions.

   Here is a sample of Pat's work on the five-step follow-up. Pat's answers are in *italic*.

Step 1   **Observation**

Review your responses to all three parts of the exercise that you have done so far.

Pat wrote: I have answered all of the questions and I can see that the form of the statements is different for each speaker, but I am not sure if the meaning is really all that different or not.

Step 2   **Selection**

Select the portions of your work that are most satisfactory and select the portions that need further attention. Find the circled segments in the transcripts. These are the areas where form differs between speakers. Notice how many of the circled areas also have underlining in them.

Count how many circles also have underlining in them and write that number here.

Pat circled almost everything in all three transcripts. This helps Pat see that the form of each person's response is different. Pat wrote that 25 of the 29 sentences were circled and underlined. This helps Pat see that the meaning is different in many cases and that differences in form have led to differences in meaning.

Step 3   **Analysis**

Analyze for accuracy. Choose any three of the illustrations and the corresponding responses to those illustrations. For example, you may choose illustration 4, 7, and 9. Examine the transcripts for the illustrations you selected. You should have a total of nine sentences to analyze, three from Diana, three from Leslie, and three from you. If you have chosen illustration 4 describe and discuss the ways in which each of the three sentences (one from each of the three speakers) succeeds or fails in transmitting the meaning contained in illustration 4. By selecting examples that are both circled and underlined, you will be able to see clearly how differences in meaning occur due to differences in form.

Pat selected sentences 4, 7, and 9 to analyze.

For sentence 4 Diana said, "She puts wooden stakes throughout the garden." Leslie said, "Now she is working with stakes putting them into the ground and patting the dirt around them." Pat said, "She staked the plants."

Pat's answer to the analysis of 4: all of these were circled except for the words "she" and "stakes." All three sentences were underlined because the meaning differs slightly in each. All three succeed in conveying the meaning conveyed by the illustration.

Step 4   **Assessment**

Select two of the three illustrations that you analyzed in step 3. Take the descriptions of successes or failures in conveying meaning from step 3 and discuss the role that form played in the success or failure in conveying the meaning as expressed by the illustrations. A failure means that meaning was lost. Differences in form that can affect meaning include omissions, additions, and a different perspective or view of what is conveyed in the illustration. Look for examples of where information that was present in the illustration was not present in the spoken version and where information that was not present in the illustration was conveyed in the spoken version. Pay special attention to where meaning was lost.

Pat selected sentence 4 in order to assess differences between form and meaning:

Diana said, "She puts wooden stakes throughout the garden." Leslie said, "Now she is working with stakes putting them into the ground and patting the dirt around them." Pat said "She staked the plants."

Pat wrote, "Diana's sentence adds that the stakes are wooden, but I am not sure that can be seen in the illustration. This is an addition at the level of form that results in a change in meaning. Diana mentioned that the staking was being done in the garden, but Leslie and I did not. That might be an omission but it does not change the meaning since the garden was mentioned earlier and is still assumed to be where she is working. None of the sentences mention that she is squatting down to do the work. This is an omission in form because this is clearly shown in the illustration. This omission affects the meaning but the meaning is not lost due to the omission. None of the sentences mention that she is using a trowel do her work. A trowel is clearly shown in the illustration so this is an omission in form that affects meaning, but the meaning is not lost.

Step 5   Action

Develop a plan for action based on your analysis and assessment. In the fifth step you review what you have discovered about your work in steps 1 through 4 and make some decisions about what steps you would like to take to improve your performance. For example, select another illustration from this unit and go through the five-step follow-up again to improve your understanding of the difference between form and meaning. You can repeat this action step until you have worked carefully with each of the nine illustrations to fully understand the difference between form and meaning.

Pat selected sentence 1 and compared all three sentences in response to the first illustration in the sequence.

Diana said, "A woman is digging in her garden." Leslie said, "There is a woman working on her garden, tilling up the soil." Pat said, "A lady is getting her garden ready to plant."

Pat wrote, "All parts are circled except 'garden' because all of the other words are different from each other. This means that there is almost no overlap in form between the three sentences. All three succeed in conveying the message shown in the illustration. My sentence does not say how she is getting the garden ready so that is an omission in form that changes the meaning of the sentence."

As a result of the follow-up, Pat realizes that the distinction between form and meaning is crucial. Pat realizes that the illustration itself is a form, that the three spoken responses to the illustration are also forms, and that the written version of the spoken English is yet another form. By carefully comparing the different sentences generated in response to a specific illustration, Pat realizes that the form chosen to express an idea can alter the meaning of the sentence.

Five Step Follow-Up

Step 1   Observation

Review your responses to all three parts of the exercise that you have completed so far. Make sure all parts are complete.

Since this type of exercise may be new to many students, encourage them to ensure that all parts of the exercise have been completed. Remind students that they are doing this exercise to better understand the differences between form and meaning.

Step 2   Selection

Find the circled segments in copy 1 of the transcript. These are the areas where form differs between you and the speakers. Count how many circles also have underlining in them and write that number here.

____

Do the same for copy 2 of the transcript.

____

The answers to this question will vary depending on how many differences between the student's work and Diana and Leslie's responses are noted by the student.

Step 3   Analysis

Using copy 1 of the transcript choose any three of the illustrations and the corresponding responses to those illustrations. For example, you may choose illustrations 4, 7, and 9. Examine the transcripts for the illustrations you selected. You should have a total of nine sentences to analyze, three from Diana, three from Leslie, and three from you. Describe and discuss the ways in which each of the three sentences (one from each of the three speakers) succeeds or fails in transmitting the meaning contained in the illustration you have selected. By selecting examples that are both circled and underlined, you will be able to see clearly how differences in meaning occur due to differences in form.

The differences in form may seem minor at first, but upon closer analysis, we see that the differences in form change the meaning. Take the example of sentence 4. Diana 4. "She puts wooden stakes throughout the garden." Leslie 4. "Now she is working with stakes, putting them into the ground and patting the dirt around them." The central meaning in both cases is that the woman placed stakes in the garden. Although both sentences convey this central idea, Leslie's sentence also adds a time frame "now" and adds "patting the dirt around them." These two elements of information change the meaning slightly.

Diana 4   "She puts wooden stakes throughout the garden."

Leslie 4   "Now she is working with stakes, putting them into the ground

and patting the dirt around them."

Step 4   Assessment

The assessment step allows you to check your understanding of the difference between form and meaning. Select two of the three illustrations that you analyzed in step 3. Take the descriptions of successes or failures in conveying meaning from step 3 and discuss the role that form played in the success or failure in conveying the meaning as expressed by the illustrations. A failure means that meaning was lost. Differences in form that can affect meaning include omissions, additions, and a different perspective or view of what is conveyed in the illustration. Look for examples where information that was present in the illustration was not present in the spoken version and where information that was not present in the illustration was conveyed in the spoken version. For each utterance determine if the meaning expressed in spoken English adds or omits information that is shown in the illustration. Write your examples of additions or omissions for each of the two illustrations here.

1. ____

____

____

2. ____

____

____

____

Look for evidence of analysis of work. It is important to be able to observe differences such as additions and omissions. These are naturally occurring differences and do not make a response "right" or "wrong." At the same time, you must be able to guide the student whose response does not convey the information in the illustration. If the student response does not convey the information in the illustration, this is an example of skewing or distorting the information presented in the illustration. This kind of error is serious and needs follow-up work until the student can accurately describe what is shown in a visual image without distorting the information. Implicit information may be included if a reason is also included. In other words, you need to ensure that the student can explain the reasoning behind the inclusion of implicit information.

Step 5   Action

Write a plan for action based on your analysis and assessment of your understanding of the difference between form and meaning. For example, select another illustration from this unit and go through the five-step follow-up again to improve your understanding of the difference between form and meaning. You can repeat this action step until you have worked carefully with each of the nine illustrations to fully understand the difference between form and meaning.

EXERCISE 1.2

Going Fishing

Please see Exercise 1.1 for instructions for the teacher.

Directions

Student Workbook
page 31

This selection is approximately three minutes long. Look at the illustrations and record your responses, listen to the speaker's responses, answer the study questions, and then do the follow-up. You need three different colored pens or pencils for this exercise, red, blue, and black. You will use these to mark on the transcripts of Diana's, Leslie's, and your own responses. Use copy 1 of the transcripts to compare your answers to Diana's and Leslie's answers. Use copy 2 of the transcripts to compare Diana's and Leslie's responses to each other. Each response is numbered. For example, Diana's first response is Diana 1 and Leslie's first response is Leslie 1. Number your responses in the same way using your own name or initials. In marking on the transcripts, a circle indicates differences in form. Underlining indicates differences in meaning.

Record and Transcribe Your Answers

Look at all nine illustrations for exercise 1.2. Record one complete sentence in spoken English on your tape recorder for each of the nine illustrations. Your sentence should include only the information that you obtain by looking at the illustration and that expresses your understanding of the illustration. Keep the context of the entire story in mind. You should not add or subtract information. Pause after each sentence and think about the information you wish to include in the next sentence.

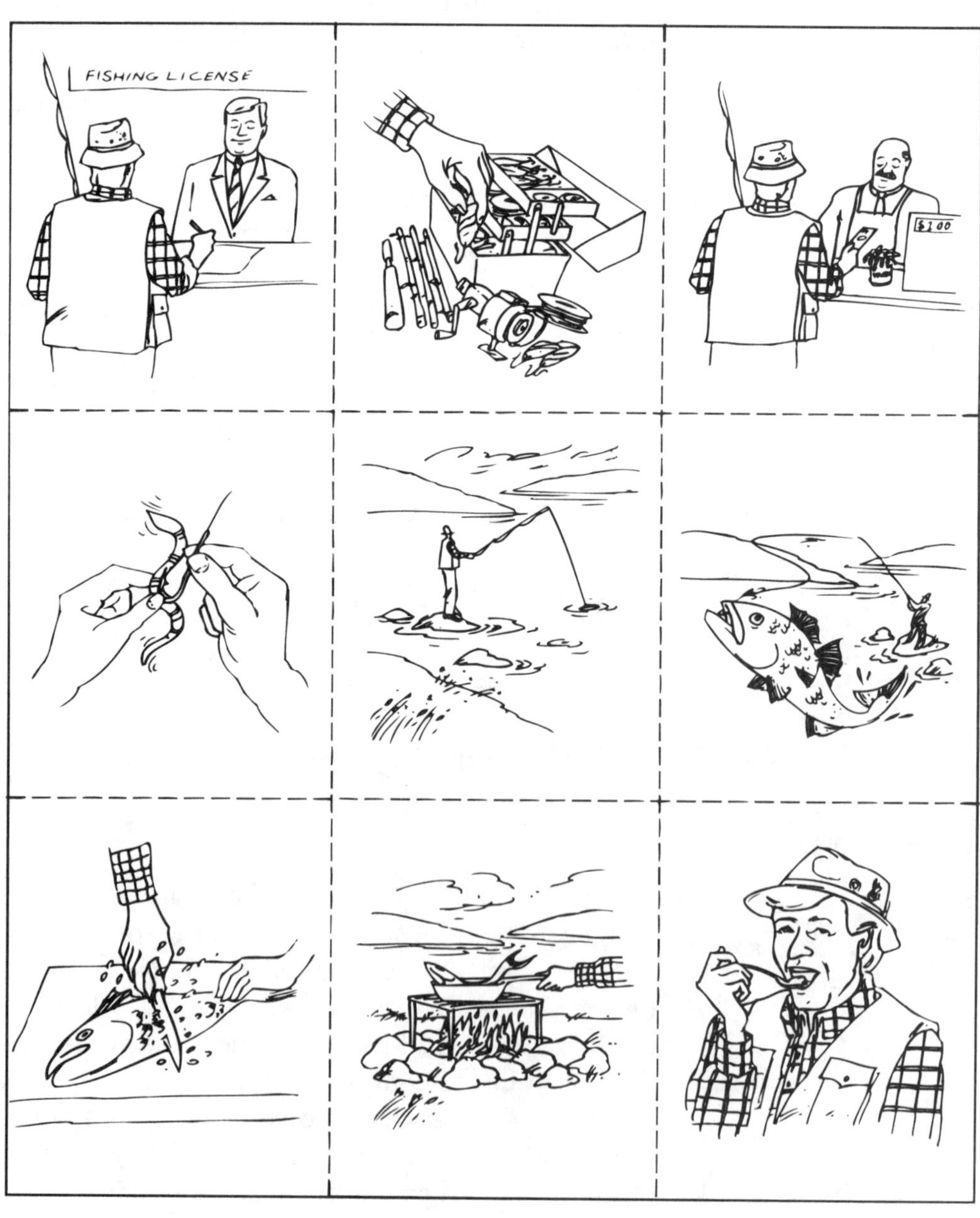

Transcribe exactly what you have recorded on your tape. This will allow you to make a direct comparison of your spoken English with the spoken English of the two speakers. Write the transcript of your responses here.

Listen to the Spoken Responses of Diana and Leslie on the Video

Transcript Copy 1 for *Going Fishing*

Diana's responses to the illustrations for going fishing:

Diana 1   A man applies for his fishing license.

Diana 2   He then puts together everything he needs for a tackle box.

Diana 3   He then pays for the tackle box.

Diana 4   He puts a worm on his hook.

Diana 5   And then he goes out into a lake and goes fishing.

Diana 6   The man catches a big fish.

Diana 7   He scales and cleans the fish.

Diana 8   Then the man cooks the fish.

Diana 9   After the fish is cooked, the man enjoys eating the fish.

Leslie's responses to the illustrations for going fishing:

Leslie 1   There is a man who has gone into a bait shop to apply for a fishing license.

Leslie 2   Now we see an open tackle box and the man pulling out a fly with a hook attached to it.

Leslie 3   He goes to the cashier to pay for the items he's selected.

Leslie 4   Now we see the man putting a worm onto the hook.

Leslie 5   Standing on a medium-sized rock he casts his line into the water.

Leslie 6   He pulls up a fish that looks bigger than he is.

Leslie 7   He takes the fish, which is actually about a foot long, and starts to scale it.

Leslie 8   Over an open pit, he roasts the fish in a frying pan.

Leslie 9   Now we see the man, in typical fashion, enjoying his fish.

Study Questions

Use red to compare your answers with Diana's. Use blue to compare your answers to Leslie's, and use black to compare Diana's and Leslie's responses to each other.

1. With regard to form, do your sentences differ from Diana's? On copy 1, circle any parts of Diana's response that differ from yours in red. Circle the corresponding difference in your response in red. For example, if your sentence is "A man is filling out a form" and Diana 1 is "A man applies for a fishing license" circle the words "filling out a form" in red in your transcript and the words "applies for a fishing license" in red in Diana's transcript.

   You can expect variations in form from each student. The student should be able to see that their own answers differ in form from Diana's.

2. With regard to form, do your sentences differ from Leslie's? On copy 1, circle any parts of Leslie's responses that differ in form from yours in blue. Circle the corresponding difference in your transcript in blue as well. Suppose your response is "A man is filling out a form" and Leslie 1 is "There is a man who has gone into a bait shop to apply for a fishing license." You would circle the entire sentence except the word "man" on your transcript. Circle all the words except "man" in blue Leslie's response. All of the other words in both sentences have a different form.

   You can expect variations in form from each student. The student should be able to see that their own answers differ in form from Leslie's.

3. With regard to meaning, do your sentences differ from Diana's? On copy 1, underline in red any parts of Diana's responses that differ from yours in meaning. Underline the corresponding section of your response in red. For example, if Diana 1 is "A man applies for a fishing license" and your response is "A man is filling out a form" you would underline in red the word "fishing license" in Diana's response and the word "form" in your response because the meaning of these two words is different. In this case you should find that the words "fishing license" and "form" already have circles around them to indicate that they do not share the

same form. Because the meaning of these words is different they should also be underlined.

Encourage students to look up any words that are circled in order to find out if the circled words are synonymous. If they are not, then the meaning is not equivalent. It is possible that the circled word could make sense but is not a synonym. You may wish to have class discussion about words that would "work" or make sense in this context, but are not synonyms.

4. With regard to meaning, do your sentences differ from Leslie's? On copy 1, underline in blue any of Leslie's responses that differ from yours in meaning. Underline the corresponding response from your transcript in blue. For example, Leslie 1 is "There is a man who has gone into a bait shop to apply for a fishing license." If your response is "A man is filling out a form" you would underline in blue the entire sentence in Leslie's transcript and the entire sentence in yours. In this case, you should find that the sentence is already circled except for "man." This should help you see that the meaning of these two sentences is different.

Encourage students to look up any words that are circled in order to find out if the circled words are synonymous. If they are not synonyms, then the meaning is not equivalent.

5. Compare Diana's and Leslie's responses to each other. Using copy 2 of the transcript of Diana's and Leslie's responses, printed below, compare Diana's and Leslie's responses with regard to form. Circle in black any words in Diana's responses that differ from Leslie's responses. Do the differences in form create differences in meaning? Write yes or no and an explanation of your answer for each utterance in the space provided following copy 2.

These comparisons should generate some lively discussion as to whether the responses are equivalent. Some suggested ways of looking at the comparisons follow copy 2.

Transcript Copy 2 for *Going Fishing*

Diana's and Leslie's responses to the illustrations for going fishing:

Diana 1   A man applies for his fishing license.

Leslie 1   There is a man who has gone into a bait shop to apply for a fishing license.

1. *Yes. Diana's utterance is in present tense, which indicates that the activity is happening now, while Leslie's indicates that it happened already. Leslie's response includes more information such as "gone into a bait shop." Although both were looking at the same illustration, each chose a different form to express what she saw. These differences in expression show that the form of the expression of the idea can actually alter the meaning slightly, or in some cases, drastically.*

Diana 2   He then puts together everything he needs for a tackle box.

Leslie 2   Now we see an open tackle box and the man pulling out a fly with a hook attached to it.

2. *Yes. The difference in form creates a difference in meaning. In Diana's response the man is putting things into a tackle box. In Leslie's response, he is taking a fly out of the box. These differences show a difference in what each speaker perceived when she looked at the illustration. It is important to emphasize that we are looking for examples of differences in form that result in a change in meaning. We are not judging the adequacy of either response, only comparing them to each other to notice the impact of form on meaning.*

Diana 3   He then pays for the tackle box.

Leslie 3   He goes to the cashier to pay for the items he's selected.

3. *Yes. The differences in form lead to differences in meaning. Leslie states explicitly where the man goes to pay (the cashier) while Diana does not.*

Leslie's response indicates that multiple items were purchased while Diana's

response indicates the purchase of a single item.

Diana 4   He puts a worm on his hook.

Leslie 4   Now we see the man putting a worm onto the hook.

4. No. The differences in form do not lead to differences in meaning. These two

utterances convey the same general meaning. Leslie's response includes the

fact that she is the observer, "Now we see the man...."

Diana 5   And then he goes out into a lake and goes fishing.

Leslie 5   Standing on a medium-sized rock he casts his line into
the water.

5. Yes. The differences in form create differences in meaning. These two

utterances convey meanings that are not equivalent. In this case, not only is

the form different, but the meaning is also different because "going out into the

lake" is not equivalent to " standing on a medium-sized rock."

Diana 6   The man catches a big fish.

Leslie 6   He pulls up a fish that looks bigger than he is.

6. *Yes. The differences in form create differences in meaning. The meanings are*
    not equivalent. They both convey the fact that the man caught a fish and that
    the fish was big. However, Leslie's response indicates that the fish is larger
    than the man while this concept of relative size is not conveyed in Diana's
    response. "Pulls up" is not synonymous with "catches."

Diana 7   He scales and cleans the fish.

Leslie 7   He takes the fish, which is actually about a foot long, and starts
to scale it.

7. *Yes. The differences in form create differences in meaning. The meanings are*
    not equivalent. Because Leslie's sentence includes information about the size of
    the fish, we cannot say that the two utterances are equivalent, but they do
    share elements that convey similar meaning indicating that the fish is being
    cleaned. Starting to scale a fish is not the same thing as cleaning and scaling
    a fish.

Diana 8   Then the man cooks the fish.

Leslie 8   Over an open pit, he roasts the fish in a frying pan.

8. *Yes. The differences in form create differences in meaning. The meaning*
    conveyed by both utterances is that the fish is cooked. Leslie's sentence adds
    information, but that addition does not skew the message. The fact that a
    frying pan was used is shown in the illustration. She did not add information

that was not in the illustration. Leslie's sentence is more specific than

Diana's sentence. You can expect discussion on this question especially

regarding "roasting" in a frying pan.

Diana 9 After the fish is cooked, the man enjoys eating the fish.

Leslie 9 Now we see the man, in typical fashion, enjoying his fish.

9. Yes. The differences in form create differences in meaning. Diana's response

includes the fact that the fish was cooked first. Leslie's response includes "in

typical fashion" and it is not clear what she means by that. This comparison

should generate some lively discussion as to whether the responses are

equivalent.

Five-Step Follow-up

See comments to the teacher in the follow-up in Exercise 1.1.

Step 1 Observation

Review your responses to all three parts of the exercise that you have done so far. Make sure all parts are complete.

Step 2 Selection

Find the circled segments in copy 1 of the transcript. These are the areas where form differs between speakers. Count how many circles also have underlining in them and write that number here.

Do the same for copy 2 of the transcript.

Step 3   **Analysis**

Using copy 1 of the transcript choose any three of the illustrations and the corresponding responses to those illustrations. For example, you may choose illustrations 3, 6, and 9. Examine the transcripts for the illustrations you selected. You have a total of nine sentences to analyze, three from Diana, three from Leslie, and three from you. Describe and discuss the ways in which each of the three sentences (one from each of the three speakers) succeeds or fails in transmitting the meaning contained in the illustration you selected. By selecting examples that are both circled and underlined, you will be able to see clearly how differences in meaning occur due to differences in form.

Step 4   **Assessment**

Select two of the three illustrations that you analyzed in step 3. Take the descriptions of successes or failures in conveying meaning from step 3 and discuss the role that form played in the success or failure in conveying the meaning as expressed by the illustrations. A failure means that meaning was lost. Differences in form that can affect meaning include omissions, additions, and a different perspective or view of what is conveyed in the illustration. Look for examples where information that was present in the illustration was not present in the spoken version and where information that was not present in the illustration was conveyed in the spoken version. For each utterance determine if the meaning expressed in spoken English adds or omits information that is shown in the illustration. Write your examples for each of the two illustrations here.

1.
____

____

____

____

2.
____

____

____

____

Step 5   **Action**

Develop a plan for action based on your analysis and assessment of your understanding of the difference between form and meaning. For example, select another illustration from this unit and go through the five-step follow-up again to improve your understanding of the difference between form and meaning. You can repeat this action step until you understand the difference between form and meaning.

____

____

____

____

____

____

____

EXERCISE 1.3

Building a Table

See instructions to the teacher in Exercise 1.1.

Directions

Student Workbook
page **40**

This selection is approximately three minutes long. Look at the illustrations and record your responses, listen to the speaker's responses, answer the study questions, and do the follow-up. You need three different colored pens or pencils for this exercise, red, blue, and black. You will use these to mark on the transcripts of Diana's, Leslie's, and your own responses. Use copy 1 of the transcripts to compare your answers to Diana's and Leslie's answers. Use copy 2 of the transcripts to compare Diana's and Leslie's responses to each other. Each response is numbered. For example, Diana's first response is Diana 1 and Leslie's first response is Leslie 1. Number your responses in the same way using your own name or initials. Use a circle to indicate differences in form. Underline to indicate differences in meaning.

Record and Transcribe Your Answers

Look at all nine illustrations for Exercise 1.3. Record one complete sentence in spoken English on your tape recorder for each of the nine illustrations. Your sentence should include only the information that you obtain by looking at the illustration and that expresses your understanding of the illustration. Keep the context of the entire story in mind. You should not add or subtract information. Pause after each sentence and think about the information you wish to include in the next sentence.

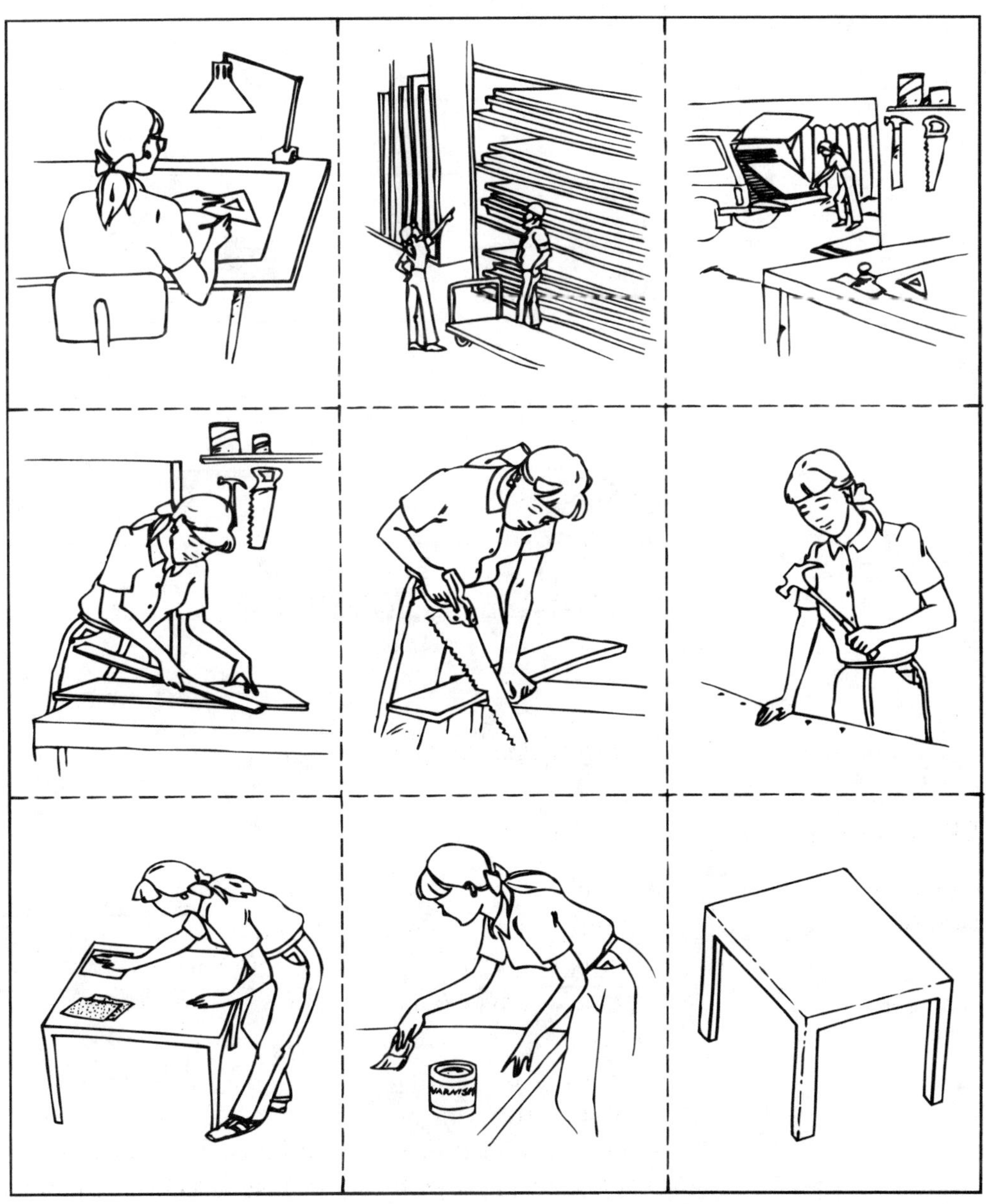

Transcribe exactly what you have recorded on your tape. This will allow you to make a direct comparison of your spoken English with the spoken English of the two speakers.

Write the transcript of your responses here.

Listen to the Spoken Responses of Diana and Leslie on the Video

Transcript Copy 1 for *Building a Table*

Diana's responses to the illustrations for building a table:

Diana 1   A woman is sitting at a desk making some plans.

Diana 2   She then goes to a store and picks out some wood.

Diana 3   She then unloads the wood from her station wagon.

Diana 4   She begins measuring the wood.

Diana 5   Then the woman cuts the wood.

Diana 6   She then hammers the nails into the wood.

Diana 7   She sands the wood with some sandpaper.

Diana 8   She then paints the wood.

Diana 9   Now she has a brand-new table.

Leslie's responses to the illustrations for building a table:

Leslie 1   First, we see a woman drafting up plans for something special.

Leslie 2   Next, she heads off to the lumberyard and picks out several select pieces of wood.

Leslie 3   She loads her purchases into the back of her pickup truck.

Leslie 4   When she gets the wood home, she starts to measure and cut.

Leslie 5   She takes a piece of wood about five feet long and makes a cut about one foot from the end.

Leslie 6   Now we see her working with a hammer, pounding the nails into the board.

Leslie 7   We see now that the project that she has completed is a small table, maybe a coffee table or end table.

Leslie 8   She puts on a coat of shellac or stain.

Leslie 9   And her project is complete.

Study Questions

Use red to compare your answers with Diana's. Use blue to compare your answers to Leslie's, and use black to compare Diana's and Leslie's responses to each other.

1. With regard to form, do your sentences differ from Diana's? On copy 1, circle any parts of Diana's response that differ from yours in red. Circle the corresponding difference in your response in red. Suppose your sentence is "A girl is drawing at a drawing table" and Diana's response Diana 1 is "A woman is sitting at a desk making some plans." Circle the entire sentence in red in your transcript and circle the entire sentence in red in Diana's transcript.

   Students should be more comfortable with the process of noting differences in form by now. You should expect to see circles on all student transcripts. If by some chance a student has listened to the video before responding to the illustrations, then the responses of Diana and Leslie could affect the student's responses and result in a closer match of form.

2. With regard to form, do your sentences differ from Leslie's? On copy 1, circle any parts of Leslie's responses that differ in form from yours in blue. Circle the corresponding difference in your transcript in blue as well. Suppose your answer is "A girl is drawing at a drawing table" and Leslie's response Leslie 1 is "First, we see a woman drafting up plans for something special." You would circle the entire sentence on your transcript. Circle the entire sentence in blue Leslie's response. There are no words except "a" that are the same in these two sentences, so the form is different with the exception of a single word.

   Remind students that meaning can still be equivalent even when form is different.

3. With regard to meaning, do your sentences differ from Diana's? On copy 1, underline in red any parts of Diana's responses that differ from yours in meaning. Underline the corresponding section of your response in red. Suppose your sentence is "A girl is drawing at a drawing table" and Diana's response Diana 1 is "A woman is sitting at a desk making some plans." Underline in red the entire sentence in Diana's response. Underline your entire response. These two sentences do not have the same

meaning. These sentences already have circles around them to indicate that they do not share the same form.

Meaning as expressed in spoken English can be quite different even when two speakers are responding to the same illustration. These differences will be the result of prior knowledge, English usage, visual acuity, and time pressures.

4. With regard to meaning, do your sentences differ from Leslie's? On copy 1, underline in blue any of Leslie's responses that differ from yours in meaning. Underline the corresponding response from your transcript in blue. For example, Leslie' response Leslie 1 "First, we see a woman drafting up plans for something special" has a different meaning than "A girl is drawing at a drawing table." Underline both of these sentences because they have different meanings. In this case, you should find that these two sentences are already circled, indicating that they do not share the same form.

Students may find that their responses are closer in either meaning or form to the responses of either Diana or Leslie. This similarity can indicate a similarity in perception between the student and the speaker and can also indicate a similarity in English expression skills. If a student response is similar to Diana's or Leslie's it does not make the response more "right." Observing the similarity is sufficient.

5. Using copy 2 of the transcript of Diana's and Leslie's responses, printed below, compare Diana's and Leslie's responses with regard to form. Circle in black any words in Diana's responses that differ from Leslie's responses. Do the differences in form create differences in meaning? Write yes or no in the space provided following copy 2.

Transcript Copy 2 for *Building a Table*

Diana's and Leslie's responses to the illustrations for building a table:

Diana 1   A woman is sitting at a desk making some plans.

Leslie 1   First, we see a woman drafting up plans for something special.

1. Yes. The difference in form creates a difference in meaning. The meaning of

these two utterances is not equivalent.

Diana 2   She then goes to a store and picks out some wood.

Leslie 2   Next, she heads off to the lumberyard and picks out several select pieces of wood.

2. *Yes. The difference in form creates a difference in meaning. Although a lumber*

   yard is a kind of store, not all stores sell lumber.

Diana 3   She then unloads the wood from her station wagon.

Leslie 3   She loads her purchases into the back of her pickup truck.

3. *Yes. The difference in form creates a difference in meaning. The meaning of*

   the two utterances is not equivalent. Loading and unloading are opposite

   concepts. A station wagon and a pick up truck are different types of vehicles.

Diana 4   She begins measuring the wood.

Leslie 4   When she gets the wood home, she starts to measure and cut.

4. *Yes. The difference in form creates a difference in meaning. The meaning of*

   the two utterances is not equivalent.

Diana 5   Then the woman cuts the wood.

Leslie 5   She takes a piece of wood about five feet long and makes a cut
about one foot from the end.

5. *Yes. The difference in form creates a difference in meaning. By now students*

   should be able to explain how the meaning is changed.

Diana 6   She then hammers the nails into the wood.

Leslie 6   Now we see her working with a hammer, pounding the nails
into the board.

6. *No. The form is different in these two utterances but the meaning is*

   essentially the same.

Diana 7   She sands the wood with some sandpaper.

Leslie 7   We see now that the project that she has completed is a small
table, maybe a coffee table or end table.

7. Yes. The difference in form creates a difference in meaning. Students should

provide rationale for their answers.

Diana 8   She then paints the wood.

Leslie 8   She puts on a coat of shellac or stain.

8. Yes. The difference in form creates a difference in meaning.

Diana 9   Now she has a brand-new table.

Leslie 9   And her project is complete.

9. Yes. The difference in form creates a difference in meaning.

Five-Step Follow-up

See the comments to the teacher in Exercise 1.1.

Step 1   Observation

Review your responses to all three parts of the exercise that you have done so far. Make sure all parts are complete.

Step 2   Selection

Find the circled segments in copy 1 of the transcripts. These are the areas where form differs between speakers. Count how many circles also have underlining in them and write that number here.

Do the same for copy 2 of the transcript.

Step 3   Analysis

Choose any three of the illustrations and the corresponding responses to those illustrations. For example, you may choose illustrations 4, 6, and 7. Examine the transcripts for the illustrations you select. You should have a total of nine sentences to analyze, three from Diana, three from Leslie, and three from you. Describe and discuss the ways in which each of the three sentences (one from each of the three speakers) succeeds or fails in transmitting the meaning contained in the illustration you have selected. By selecting examples that are both circled and underlined, you will be able to see clearly how differences in meaning occur due to differences in form.

____

____

____

____

____

____

____

Step 4   Assessment

Select two of the three illustrations that you analyzed in step 3. Take the descriptions of successes or failures in conveying meaning from step 3 and discuss the role that form played in the success or failure in conveying the meaning as expressed by the illustrations. A failure means that meaning was lost. Differences in form that can affect meaning include omissions, additions, and a different perspective or view of what is conveyed in the illustration. Look for examples where information that was present in the illustration was not present in the spoken version and where information that was not present in the illustration was conveyed in the spoken version. For each utterance determine if the meaning expressed in spoken English adds or omits information that is shown in the illustration. Write your examples for each of the two illustrations here.

1. ____

____

____

2. _______________________________

Step 5   Action

Develop a plan for action based on your analysis and assessment of your understanding of the difference between form and meaning. For example, select another illustration from this unit and go through the five-step follow-up again to improve your understanding of the difference between form and meaning. You can repeat this action step until you have worked carefully with each of the nine illustrations to fully understand the difference between form and meaning.

Additional Exercises at the Sentence Level to Compare Form and Meaning

1. Use the sentences you created and change them to negative sentences. How does this change in form affect the meaning of each sentence?

This exercise should be fairly easy for most students. Students can do it out loud in a group format. This is a good way to emphasize how a change in form can change the meaning.

2. Change the negated sentences into questions. How does this change in form affect the meaning of the sentences? How does the meaning compare with the original sentence that you created?

This exercise builds on the previous one. It is a good exercise to see if students can manage negation and question forms and still evaluate how these changes in form affect meaning.

Progress Tracking Sheet

This sheet is designed to help you keep track of which exercises you have completed and how well you have done on these exercises. See page 13 (Teacher's Guide page 20) for a full description of how to use the Progress Tracking Sheet.

Exercise Number	Date	First Performance	Study Questions	Follow-up Activity	Questions and Reminders	Date	Second Performance
Exercise 1.1 Quantitative							
Qualitative							
Exercise 1.2 Quantitative							
Qualitative							
Exercise 1.3 Quantitative							
Qualitative							
Quantitative Totals							

Meaning and Visual Form

Introduction

There are two goals for this unit. The first is to highlight the difference between meaning conveyed in spoken English form and in visual form (illustrations). The second is to develop visualization as a specific tool in the interpretation process. There are five factors to consider with regard to form and meaning. The four forms in this unit are (1) the illustration, (2) the spoken English, (3) the transcription of the spoken English, and (4) a visualization created in response to the spoken English and then (5) the meaning that these four forms share. This unit emphasizes the fact that the form of a message can take various shapes while the meaning can remain constant.

This unit includes practice in listening to spoken English and creating an image, either on paper or solely in the mind. Nancy Schweda Nicholson (1996) calls the place where images are created in the mind's eye the "visuospatial sketchpad." The visuospatial sketchpad is an important tool for interpreters to develop and use effectively. Often, when an image is visualized, it is remembered better. Sometimes visualization can help in setting up spatial relationships between objects or people referred to in the discourse.

In the video for this unit, Diana and Leslie looked at the same illustrations and provided English sentences in response to what they saw. You will listen to their spoken English sentences and create your own visualization based on what you heard. Then you will compare your visualization with the illustration that the speakers were looking at when they created their sentences.

Group discussions after the exercises will reveal that there are almost as many different visualizations as there are participants. Some of those differences will be based on assumptions and some will be based on what was actually said. Sometimes these differences will be due to implicit and explicit information and the ways in which the speakers deal with these types of information. The main topics for this unit are visualization, nonlinguistic visual form, spoken form, meaning, and implicit and explicit information.

Visualization

Visualization is the creation of a "scene" or picture in your mind's eye. This is the process that allows you to hear a message in English and imagine where the items or persons are located in relation to each other. This skill has three important components. One is visualizing the relationships between things or people that you already know, but that are not visible at that moment. The second component is imagining relationships between items or people when you have no prior visual knowledge of their spatial relationships. An example of this difference can be seen in imagining yourself interpreting directions from point A to point B when you already know the way and interpreting the same directions when you have never seen either point A or point B or any of the points in between. Visualization is a way to give form to a scene that you know but cannot see, or to give form to a scene that you imagine. Once you have established this form in your mind's eye, you refer to it as you proceed through the interpretation. If visualization is done correctly, then the person you have referred to as being on your right remains there throughout the interpretation. Likewise, the other objects or persons which are being spoken about have "assigned places" in your mind and in your interpretation. The third component relies on visual memory of a scene that you have seen. You "remember" this scene by using the visuo–spatial sketchpad.

Visual Form

Visual form refers to the graphic images that are shown in this unit. The illustrations do not have any specific language form attached to them.

Spoken Form

For these exercises, the spoken form is the English generated in response to the visual form. The spoken form is on the videotape. The spoken form serves as the basis for the written form that is the transcript. The English that is shown in the transcription is an exact representation of what Diana and Leslie said in response to the illustrations.

Meaning

The concept of meaning is extremely complex and is not dealt with in depth here. Refer to Seleskovitch and Lederer (1989) or other authors who write about meaning as it relates to interpretation. Gonzalez et al. (1991) provide a good description of the role of meaning in the interpretation process. In brief, the concepts that underlie the spoken form or the visual form constitute the meaning Seleskovitch and Lederer (1989) refer to meaning as the "sense" of a message. Meaning is the idea or concept that one person wishes to convey to another or that is conveyed by an illustration or imagined in a visualization.

Implicit and Explicit Information

According to Larson (1984), "Explicit information is information that is overtly stated by lexical items and grammatical forms" (p. 38). Implicit information is information which is understood but not necessarily overtly stated. Information may be implicit because of shared prior information or it may be due to the structure of the language.

Interpreters often wonder how much "explaining" is appropriate during the interpretation process. At issue here is information that is clearly understood and available to native speakers of the source language but that speakers of the target language might not understand. The implicit information could be culturally bound information or it could be information that people share due to a shared history in dealing with a specific subject. If the people involved in the conversation share the same history and understanding of the topic, then the implicit information does not need to be made explicit.

Larson (1984) offers the following explanation of implicit information. Some information is implicit due to the structure of the language and some information is implicit due to prior knowledge. "Implicit information is part of the meaning which is to be communicated by the translation because it is part of the meaning intended to be understood by the original writer" (p. 38). An example of implicit information based on prior knowledge is seen in the sentence "When I entered college, I decided to be a physics major but I decided if I wanted to graduate on time, I should change my major to something else." Implicit in this sentence is that it might take longer to complete a degree in physics than in some other subject. Interpreters need to develop the skill of discerning which information is implicit and which is explicit so that their interpretations will be accurate.

The Role of Creating Visual Forms in Response to Spoken Information in the Interpretation Process

Interpreters work between spoken languages or between signed and spoken languages. Schweda Nicholson (1996) says that the visuospatial sketchpad is a construct that can assist in developing memory and accuracy in interpretation. To do this, the interpreter must hear the incoming message or source language and perform various mental manipulations to free the message from its original form. One way to do this is to create a visual image.

Sometimes you do not know whether the object the speaker is referring to is to the right or left of the speaker. It can be crucial to know the actual location of objects or persons in relation to each other, and other times it is sufficient to know simply that things are in relation to each other. If you sense that the exact relationship is important, then you may need to ask the speaker for clarification. Examples of instances in which this kind of information is essential could include situations where directions are being given to create something, such as a recipe or a building plan. Another instance in which it is important to know the actual relationship is legal testimony, where the exact relationship and location of persons and objects can be very important.

The material in this unit encourages you to realize that you automatically visualize situations without realizing it and that the visualizations may or may not match the actual event being spoken about. It is as if your mind constantly creates hypotheses about what the speaker means and about what the speaker might say. While the creation of hypotheses is important, it is also important to realize that not all hypotheses will actually be borne out. It is a mark of a skilled interpreter to realize that there may be more than one possible hypothesis and that one or more may need to be discarded in order to convey the meaning intended by the speaker.

Discussion Questions

Discuss the following questions with your students to promote insight and increase awareness of the role of visualization in the interpretation process.

1. *How does visualization relate to the interpretation process?*

    Students should be able to answer this question based on the reading in this chapter. Visualization is crucial to the interpretation process and it is important to take time to encourage students to develop this skill. Creating a visual image in response to a spoken message can be a powerful tool to aid the interpreter's memory. It is easier for the interpreter to create and remember a visual image than try to remember all the words they just heard. It is important that the interpreter remember what was just said, as the interpreter cannot interpret what he or she cannot remember. Visualizing the relationships between actors and objects can be a great asset for the interpreter. Accurate visualization skills combined with memory skills reduce the effort needed for the process and reduce the errors in the product.

2. *Do you feel you can visualize everything you hear?*

    People often do not really attend to what they are hearing and as a result do not often try to visualize accurately. However, people tend to think they have heard and visualized correctly. Encourage students to realize that the kind of visualization and memory skills used in everyday conversations are not the same as the level of intense visualization and memory that must be used in the inter-

pretation process. The first step in accurate visualization is intense, effortful listening. Visualization is not an innate process, but it can be learned and developed with specific effort. By developing this skill, less effort will be needed later during the more demanding process of simultaneous interpretation.

3. *What happens when the interpreter does not visualize the message correctly, but thinks that he or she has visualized correctly?*

    The product will most likely be skewed and the interpreter will not realize it. It is possible that an inaccurate visualization will not affect the message. In some cases the actual location of the objects or actors referred to will be inconsequential. It may not matter that Mr. Jones was on Mr. Smith's left and the interpreter visualized Mr. Jones on Mr. Smith's right. However, the interpreter cannot know in advance if the location of the actors and objects in the discourse is crucial or not. It is best to bring this kind of possible discrepancy to the attention of your students and encourage them to note that this kind of discrepancy or ambiguity can lead to a skewed interpretation and that it is best to ask for clarification, when possible. Alternatively, a neutral solution such as "the men stood next to each other" may be the best option.

4. *What happens when the interpreter does not correctly visualize the spoken message and he or she realizes that they have not correctly visualized the message?*

    Ideally the interpreter will stop the speaker and ask for a repetition. Encourage students to realize that it is common to gain understanding of the relationships between actors and objects and events during the interpretation process. It is possible and likely that an interpreter's understanding of the crucial relationships in a discourse can change as he or she becomes more familiar with the events as described by the speaker. If the interpreter has misunderstood based on a faulty visualization, then the interpreter can create a repair, or revised interpretation of the crucial aspects of the relationship. This kind of repair "midstream" may require the interpreter to interrupt the speaker momentarily to have time to create the repair.

Meaning and Visual Form Exercises

Decide if you want to conduct these exercises in class, or if you want the students to do the exercises on their own time. If students do the exercises on their own, they must have their own source tape. The exercises can be done in a group setting. Students respond by writing or drawing.

If you decide to conduct the exercises during class time, be sure all the students can see the TV monitor you are using. Check to see that the volume is appropriate for the number of students in the room. Ask the students to prepare themselves to listen carefully. Remind them not to write or draw while listening. Ask all students to refrain from making noise while the tape is being played.

Read the directions and explain them to the students. Allow time for questions after you have given the directions. You should plan at least five minutes to prepare the students for each exercise. Five minutes should be enough, if you have the group's attention, and if all equipment is ready and in working order. All tapes needed for these exercises must be cued to the correct spot. This includes the source tape and any tapes that will be used for recording.

The exercises in this unit are designed to increase awareness of the importance of visualization and the difference between implicit and explicit information. Some of the information conveyed by the illustrations may be assumed to be implicit by some speakers and may need to be made explicit by other speakers. Examples of differences regarding implicit information appear in Diana's and Leslie's responses to the illustrations.

In these exercises, the goal is to clarify the difference between form and meaning, when the form presented is the spoken English form of a message.

There are five factors in the exercises:
1. The illustration or visual form.
2. The visualization derived from that illustration.
3. The spoken English form.
4. The transcript of the spoken English form.
5. The meaning that these four forms share.

Two different native speakers of English were instructed to create an utterance or sentence that conveys the meaning shown in the illustration or visual form. Each of the speaker's utterances is transcribed into written English. The visual form that the speakers looked at is shown in each exercise. You will create your own visual form (visualization) as you listen to the spoken English. Later, as you compare your visualizations to the illustrations, it will become clear that the meaning of the illustrations can and will be expressed in slightly different forms, depending on the way a person chooses to speak English.

Even though you and the two speakers are all looking at the same illustrations, it is unlikely that any two sentences or any two visualizations for a specific illustration will be exactly the same. Thus, the form is different, and the meaning remains constant. It is true that variations in expression can slightly alter the meaning. The amount of difference in meaning is one of the judgements you will be asked to make as you work through the exercises. These short scenarios do not contain contextual or cultural information. Additional context can be created in order to add more variety to these exercises.

The two speakers chosen for these exercises have much in common, such as gender, approximate age range, and educational level. Despite these similarities, you will see that the forms chosen to express the meanings they understood are quite distinct. Neither speaker rehearsed their responses in advance of the taping. This allowed for a more spontaneous rendition of the meaning as each person saw it. Please note that neither version is considered "right"; rather, each spoken sentence represents the speakers' view and manner of expression.

As you practice your visualization skills based only on what you hear, you will notice that sometimes the details that you create in your mind's eye can vary depending on your visualization skills. Sometimes, details that cannot be determined from the illustrations are added. This kind of addition is usually based on assumptions. It is important to create a visualization that is as accurate as possible so as not to skew or distort the message. Another common error is to leave out information that was stated. For example, the speaker may say "The coffee shop is just inside the door to the mall." Your visualization should include an image of a mall with the coffee shop at the door, not an image of a coffee shop on the corner. These kinds of additions and omissions are common. Sometimes they are minor and do not create a significant difference in the meaning. You will need to decide if any of these omissions or additions substantially change the meaning of the messages that you will be working with in this unit.

EXERCISE 2.1

Doing the Laundry

Directions

Student Workbook
page 56

This selection is approximately three minutes long. Listen to the video selection, answer the study questions, and then do the follow-up. You will need three different colored pens or pencils for this exercise, red, blue, and black. You will use these to mark differences that you find between your visualizations, the illustrations, and the transcripts. Each of the speaker's responses is numbered for easy reference. For example, Diana's first response is Diana 1 and Leslie's first response is Leslie 1. Read all of the directions, then begin work on the first part of the exercise.

Create Your Visualizations

Find this selection on your videotape. Do not look at the printed illustrations before you create your visualization. Listen as Leslie describes each of the nine illustrations in the sequence. Visualize what she is describing. You can create a mental visualization or draw a quick sketch that represents what you hear her say. Keep track of the spatial relationships between actors and objects she describes. Do not worry about your artistic ability, simply make a quick line drawing. Stick figures are fine. Do not write or say any English words to help you remember what she said. Stop the tape after each sentence when you hear the beep to give yourself enough time to create your visualization. You can draw while listening. Then, listen to Diana describe the same set of nine illustrations. Visualize or draw a quick sketch representing what you heard her say. Keep track of the spatial relationships between actors and objects she describes. Do not use written or spoken English to help you remember what she said.

Visualizations Based on Leslie's Responses

1	2	3
4	5	6
7	8	9

Visualizations Based on Diana's Responses

1	2	3
4	5	6
7	8	9

Study Questions

1. Compare your visualizations or drawings created in response to Leslie's sentences with the illustrations on page 61 (Teacher's Guide, page 77). Look at each of the illustrations. In each illustration (not your visualization) circle in blue any differences between your visualization and the illustration. The differences might be due to information that is either missing or added by the speaker or due to information that you assumed was included, but was not. For each of the nine illustrations decide if the meaning of your visualization is the same or different from the illustration. Write "same" or "different" in the numbered spaces below. For example, if you visualized that the laundry was already in the basement rather than being carried, you would circle the laundry basket in the man's arms in blue and write "different" in space 1.

    Note: The general notes to the teacher appear in the first set of study questions. Additional comments for Exercises 2.2 and 2.3 are included only if necessary.

    In working with students on this question and the one that follows, avoid discussions of drawing ability or lack of drawing ability. If the student responds quickly to the spoken English and moves to these study questions directly, they should be able to remember what image they were able to create in their mind's eye, regardless of whether they were able to draw it. Next, the student should compare the visual image in their mind's eye and the visual image presented in the book. The visual image they create on paper should be a prompt or cue to help them remember what they visualized. It is important to avoid using written English as a visual prompt. The idea is to see what kind of access the student has to creating a nonlinguistic or pictorial image in their mind's eye in response to a spoken English message. To promote discussion about the differences the students found between their visualizations and the illustration, ask them to provide short descriptions of the differences they noted. These descriptions can be written or can be part of an in-class discussion.

    1. ___________________________________

    2. ___________________________________

    3. ___________________________________

    4. ___________________________________

    5. ___________________________________

    6. ___________________________________

    7. ___________________________________

8. ___________________________

9. ___________________________

2. Compare your visualizations or drawings created in response to Diana's sentences with the illustrations on page 61 (Teacher's Guide page 77). Look at each of the illustrations. In each illustration circle in red any differences between your visualization and the illustration. The differences might be due to information that is either missing or added by the speaker or to information that you assumed was included, but was not. For each of the nine illustrations decide if the meaning of your visualization is different from the illustration. Write "different" in the corresponding numbered spaces below. For example, Diana's response to the first illustration is "A man brings his laundry downstairs." If your visualization did not include a laundry basket, circle the laundry basket in red and write "different" in space 1 below.

1. ___________________________

2. ___________________________

3. ___________________________

4. ___________________________

5. ___________________________

6. ___________________________

7. ___________________________

8. ___________________________

9. ___________________________

3. Using your answers to question 1, select the illustrations that you have marked as being different in meaning from your visualization. For each one of these differences, refer to the transcript of Leslie's spoken English and determine which part of her utterance led you to create a visualization that differed in meaning from the original illustration and underline it in black. For example, in Leslie's first sentence, she says, "There is a man heading down the basement steps to put his clothes in the laundry." If you envisioned that the laundry was already in the basement then you

might underline the transcript like this, "There is a man <u>heading</u> down the basement steps <u>to put</u> his clothes in the laundry." The word "heading" might create in your mind a visualization that he is walking downstairs empty-handed. Select the portion of the sentence whose meaning led you to create a visualization that differed from the illustration.

The goal of this question and the one that follows is to encourage students to gain insight as to why they formed the visualization they did. Was the visualization actually based on something they heard or something they assumed they heard. Was it based on implicit or explicit information? Did the student listen carefully to what was explicitly stated? What role did prior knowledge play in forming a visualization, if any?

4. Using your answers to question 2, select the illustrations that you have marked as being different in meaning from your visualization. For each one of these differences, refer to the transcript of Diana's spoken English and determine which part of her utterance led you to create a visualization that differed in meaning from the original illustration and underline it in black. For example, in Diana's first sentence, she says "A man brings his laundry downstairs." If you envisioned that he carried the laundry in his arms and not in a basket, you would underline the word "brings" because your understanding of the meaning of "brings" led you to a visualization that was different from the illustration.

5. Read the transcript of Leslie's responses and compare it to the illustrations it describes. Underline in blue any information in the transcript that is not in the illustrations. Your visualization is based on what you heard and should contain the same additions.

This question and the one that follows are designed to encourage students to evaluate the effects of additions. If the student does not include all of the spoken information in the visualization, what are the effects on the message that is interpreted based on the visualization? Naturally, the product of the interpretation will also contain additions. Next, it is important to evaluate the seriousness of the effect of the additions on the overall product. This exercise helps students to see that it is crucial to include all the information without adding extraneous information.

6. Read the transcript of Diana's responses and compare it to the illustrations it describes. Underline in red any information in the transcript that is not in the illustration. Your visualization is based on what you heard and should contain the same additions.

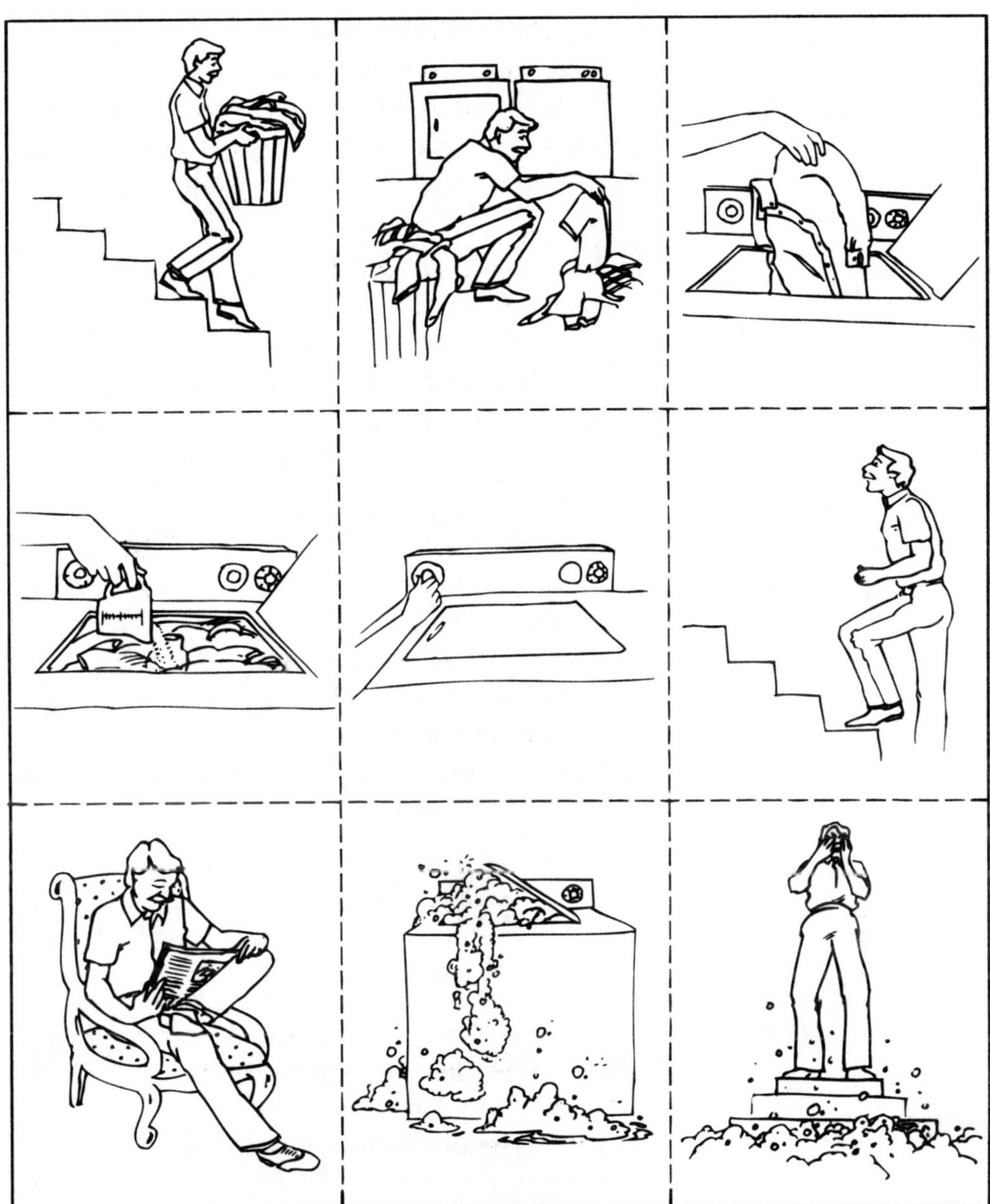

Transcript *Doing the Laundry*

Leslie's responses to the illustrations for doing the laundry:

Leslie 1   There is a man heading down the basement steps to put his clothes in the laundry.

Leslie 2   On the basement floor, he separates the clothes out, whites and darks.

Leslie 3   He puts his clothes in the washer.

Leslie 4   Then he adds a cup of detergent.

Leslie 5   Next, he closes the lid and turns the machine on.

Leslie 6   He heads back upstairs.

Leslie 7   Then he sits down in a comfy armchair to enjoy a magazine or newspaper.

Leslie 8   Meanwhile, the washer is overflowing with suds and water.

Leslie 9   By the time he heads downstairs, the suds have come halfway up the basement stairs.

Diana's responses to the illustrations:

Diana 1   A man brings his laundry downstairs.

Diana 2   When he gets downstairs, he sorts his laundry.

Diana 3   He then puts his shirts into the washing machine.

Diana 4   He pours soap into the machine.

Diana 5   He then turns the machine on.

Diana 6   The man walks back up the stairs.

Diana 7   He sits down and begins reading a newspaper.

Diana 8   In the laundry room, soap is overflowing from the washing machine.

Diana 9   When the man gets back downstairs he is horrified to see soap all over the floor.

Five-Step Follow-up

Step 1   Observation

Review your responses to all 3 parts of the exercise that you have done so far. Make sure all parts are complete.

Encourage students to complete all parts of the exercises. This kind of exercise may be a new experience for many students. They are being asked to grasp yet another way that form and meaning differ. Some students may not have had prior experiences with visualization. It is important that they complete all parts of the exercise prior to this point before going on.

Step 2   Selection

Refer to your answers to study questions 3 and 4. These are the places where you noted that your visualization did not match the illustration itself. You have already underlined the portions of the transcript of Leslie's and Diana's responses that may have led you to a different meaning than that shown in the illustration. Select three of these sentences from each speaker's transcript to analyze in the next step.

If a student does not have any instances in which the visualization does not match the illustration (this is unlikely), ask them to pick the three sentences that they found most confusing.

Step 3   Analysis

Explain how the underlined sections of the transcript affected your understanding of the meaning. For example, in Diana 4, "He pours soap into the machine," you may have underlined "soap" because you envisioned that it was liquid laundry detergent while the illustration shows that it might be powdered soap. Analyze what effect assumptions had on your visualizations. In some cases what you assumed to be true may not have been included in what the speaker said. Finally, indicate which sentences from each of the two transcripts succeeds or fails in transmitting the meaning contained in the illustration.

Use this space to write your explanation for the underlined sections in three sentences from Diana's transcript that you have chosen to analyze.

For this question and the one that follows, encourage students to be detail-oriented. Point out how small details can make a difference in the overall meaning. This is the place to really delve into the answers and the results of the understandings and misunderstandings and how these affect the visualization process. Allow time for class discussion.

Sample:

Diana 2   When he gets downstairs he sorts his laundry.

I assumed that sorting the laundry would result in three piles of clothes, light, dark, and white. Since the illustration does not show three piles, my visualization includes an assumption that adds information that was not stated or shown in the illustration. The speaker has succeeded in conveying the information shown in the illustration.

Use this space for your analysis of Diana's responses.

1. ____

____

2. ____

____

3. ____

____

Use this space for your analysis of Leslie's responses.

1. ____

____

2. ____

____

3. ____

____

Leslie's responses had a different form than Diana's. Did the form of Leslie's responses affect the visualizations that you created in response to Diana's sentences? Describe three examples where this happened.

1. ____

____

2. ____

____

3. ____

____

This section encourages students to keep in mind the effect of form on meaning.

Step 4   Assessment

Select three of the six illustrations that you analyzed in step 3. Take the descriptions of successes or failures in conveying meaning from step 3 and discuss the role that visualization played in the success or failure in understanding the meaning as expressed by the speaker and the illustrations. A failure means that meaning was lost. This would mean that you envisioned an illustration that was substantially different from the illustration shown in the workbook. Remember that your visualizations are based on what you hear and that what you hear is based on what that speaker understood from the illustration. Each speaker provides you with a different form to listen to. Differences in form that can affect meaning include omissions, additions, and a different perspective or view of what is conveyed in the illustration. Look for examples where information that was present in the illustration was not present in the spoken version and where information that was not present in the illustration was conveyed in the spoken version.

1. ____

____

2. ____

____

3. ____

____

Here we are looking for an explicit description from the student that shows they have a grasp on the difference between form and meaning, how the visualization process fits into the interpretation process, and how visualization can affect both form and meaning. You may need to help students find the language to express their understanding.

Step 5   Action

Develop a plan for action based on your analysis and assessment of your understanding of the importance of visualizing and the difference between form and meaning. For example, select another illustration from this unit and go through the five-step follow-up again to improve your understanding of the difference between form and meaning. You can repeat this action step until you have worked carefully with each of the nine illustrations to fully understand the role of visualization and the difference between form and meaning.

____

____

____

____

____

____

This step is especially important for any student who has not demonstrated a clear grasp of the ideas and processes in this exercise. This step can also be used as a refresher at a later time, say between semesters, when students may have more time to work on this process and help solidify it for themselves.

EXERCISE 2.2

Making a Cake

See directions and notes to the teacher in Exercise 2.1

Directions

**Student Workbook
page 66**

This selection is approximately three minutes long. Listen to and watch the video selection, answer the study questions, and then do the follow-up. You will need three different colored pens or pencils for this exercise, red, blue, and black. You will use these to mark differences that you find between your visualizations, the illustrations, and the transcripts. Each of the speaker's responses is numbered for easy reference. For example, Diana's first response is Diana 1, and Leslie's first response is Leslie 1.

Create Your Visualizations

Find this selection on your videotape. Do not look at the printed illustrations yet. Listen to Leslie describe each of the eight illustrations in the sequence. Visualize the images she is describing. Create a mental visualization or draw a quick sketch that represents what you heard her say. Keep track of the spatial relationships between the actors and objects she describes. Do not worry about your artistic ability, simply make a quick line drawing. Do not write or say any English words to help you remember what she said. Stop the tape after each sentence when you hear the beep to give yourself enough time to create your visualization. Then, listen to Diana describe the same set of eight illustrations. Visualize or draw a quick sketch representing what you heard her say. Keep track of the spatial relationships between the actors and objects she describes. You can draw while listening. Do not use written or spoken English to help you remember what she said. Stop the tape at the end of this selection.

Visualizations Based on Leslie's Responses

<table>
<tr><td>1</td><td>2</td></tr>
<tr><td>3</td><td>4</td></tr>
<tr><td>5</td><td>6</td></tr>
<tr><td>7</td><td>8</td></tr>
</table>

Visualizations Based on Dianas Responses

1	2
3	4
5	6
7	8

Study Questions

1. Compare your visualizations or drawings created in response to Leslie's sentences with the illustrations on page 71 (Teacher's Guide page 88). Look at each of the illustrations. In each illustration circle in blue any differences between your visualization and the illustration. The differences might be due to information that is either missing or added by the

speaker or to information that you assumed was included, but was not. For each of the eight illustrations decide if the meaning of your visualization is the same or different from the illustration. Write "same" or "different" in the corresponding numbered spaces below. For example, Leslie's response to the first illustration is "There is a woman looking in a cookbook and envisioning a great–looking layered cake." If your visualization did not include a cookbook, circle the cookbook in blue to show the difference in form. Then write "different" in space 1 below.

Note that the two speakers had different ideas about what happened in this sequence of illustrations. This difference in perception of what was shown in the illustrations led to differences in the spoken English. The differences in the spoken English will lead to differences in the visualizations. Here is a good opportunity to see if students are influenced by what the first speaker said while listening to the second speaker. The student may expect the story line to be about the same in both cases, but the story lines are different.

1. _______________________________

2. _______________________________

3. _______________________________

4. _______________________________

5. _______________________________

6. _______________________________

7. _______________________________

8. _______________________________

2. Compare your visualizations or drawings created in response to Diana's sentences with the illustrations on page 71 (Teacher's Guide page 88). Look at each of the illustrations. In each illustration circle in red any differences between your visualization and the illustration. The differences might be due to information that is either missing or added by the speaker or to information that you assumed was included, but was not. For each of the eight illustrations decide if the meaning of your visualization is the same or different from the illustration. Write "same" or "different" in the numbered spaces below. Diana's response to the first illustration is "A woman gets out a cookbook and decides to make a cake." If your visualization did not include a cookbook, circle the cookbook in red and then write "different" in space 1 below.

1. _______________________________

2. _______________________________

3. _______________________________

4. _______________________________

5. _______________________________

6. _______________________________

7. _______________________________

8. _______________________________

3. Using your answers to question 1, select the illustrations that you have marked as being different in meaning from your visualization. For each of these differences, refer to the transcript of Leslie's spoken English and determine which part of the utterance led you to create a visualization that differed in meaning from the original illustration and underline it in black. For example, in Leslie's first sentence, she says, "There is a woman looking in a cookbook and envisioning a great-looking layered cake." If you envisioned that the cake had six layers, then you might underline the word "great" in the transcript because that might create in your mind a visualization that the cake has many layers. Select the portion of the sentence whose meaning led you to create a visualization that differed from the illustration.

4. Using your answers to question 2, select the illustrations that you have marked as being different in meaning from your visualization. For each of these differences, refer to the transcript of Diana's spoken English and determine which part of the utterance led you to create a visualization that differed in meaning from the original illustration and underline it in black. Underline the word(s) that led you to a visualization that was different from the illustration.

5. Read the transcript of Leslie's responses and compare it to the illustrations it describes. Underline in blue any information in the transcript that is not in the illustrations. Your visualization is based on what you heard and should contain the same additions.

6. Read the transcript of Diana's responses and compare it to the illustrations it describes. Underline in red any information in the transcript that is not in the illustrations. Your visualization is based on what you heard and should contain the same additions.

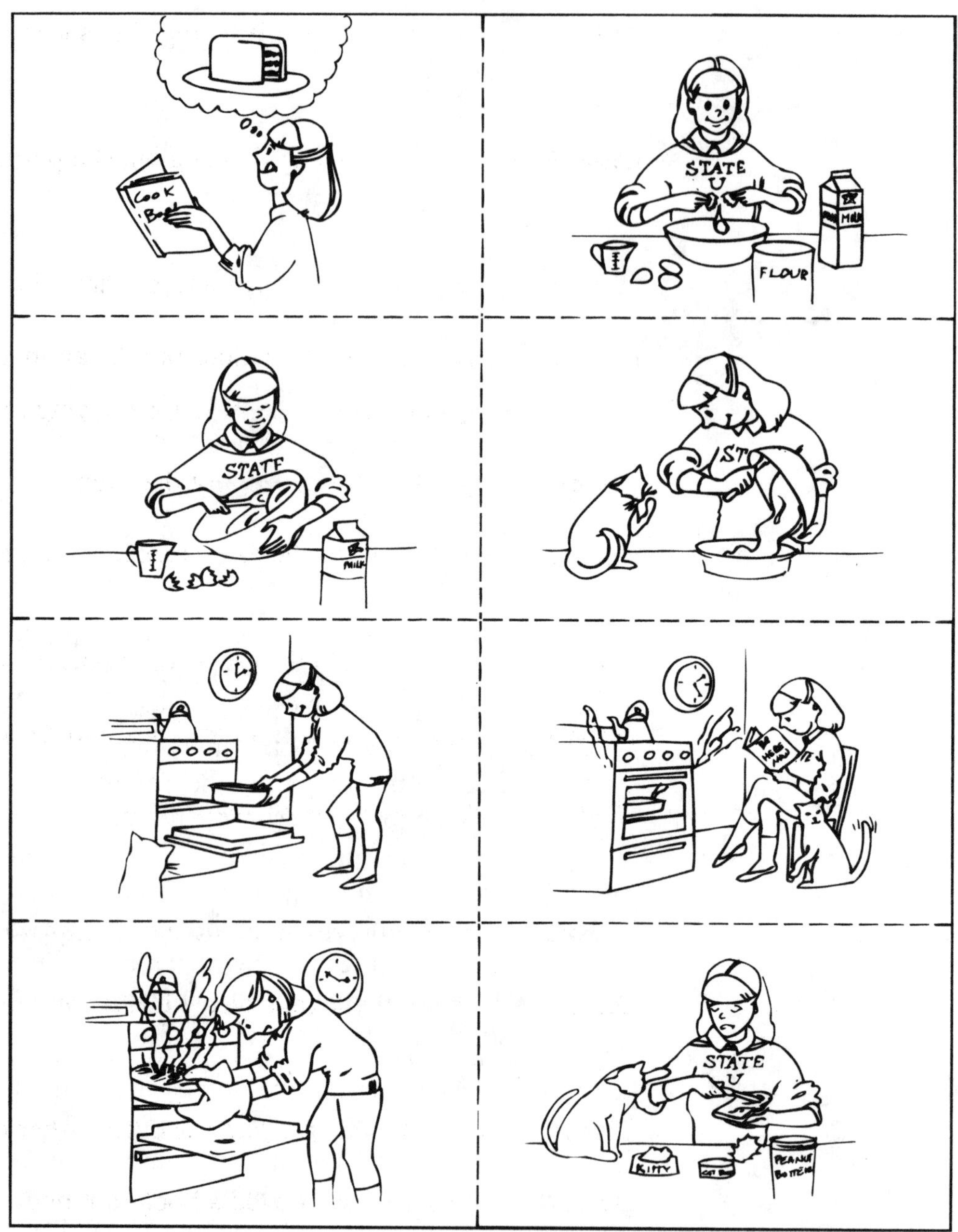

Transcript for *Making a Cake*

Leslie's responses to the illustrations for making a cake:

Leslie 1   There is a woman looking in a cookbook and envisioning a great-looking layered cake.

Leslie 2   She gets her ingredients together and cracks some eggs into a large bowl.

Leslie 3   With all the ingredients together she stirs the thick batter with a wooden spoon.

Leslie 4   Then, with her cat looking on, she pours the batter into a cake pan.

Leslie 5   She puts the cake pan into the heated oven.

Leslie 6   She closes the oven door but the aromas are able to waft out and she and the cat sit there enjoying them.

Leslie 7   She takes the cake out of the oven.

Leslie 8   Before frosting the cake she slices up a nice piece for kitty.

Diana's responses to the illustrations for making a cake:

Diana 1   A woman gets out a cookbook and decides to make a cake.

Diana 2   She gets out all the ingredients she needs, including flour, eggs, and milk.

Diana 3   She then mixes all of the ingredients in a bowl.

Diana 4   She pours the ingredients into a pan while her cat licks his paws.

Diana 5   She puts the cake into the oven, as her cat looks on.

Diana 6   She sits down to read a book, not noticing that smoke is pouring out of the oven. Her cat nervously wiggles his tail.

Diana 7   She takes the burned cake out of the oven.

Diana 8   The woman makes herself a peanut butter sandwich and gives her cat some cat food.

Five-Step Follow-up

Step 1   Observation

Review your responses to all parts of the exercise that you have done so far. Make sure all parts are complete.

Step 2   Selection

Refer to your answers to study questions 3 and 4. These are the places where you noted that your visualization did not match the illustration itself. You have already underlined the portions of the transcript of Leslie's and Diana's responses that may have created a meaning different than that shown in the illustration. Select three sentences from each speaker's transcript to analyze in the next step.

Step 3   Analysis

Explain how the underlined sections of the transcript affected your understanding of the meaning. For example, Diana 1 is "A woman gets out a cookbook and decides to make a cake." You may have underlined "cake" because you may have visualized a square cake in a pan. Analyze the effect assumptions had on your visualizations. In some cases what you assumed to be true may not have been included in what the speaker said. Finally, indicate which sentences from each of the two transcripts succeeds or fails in transmitting the meaning contained in the illustration. Use the spaces provided below to write your answers for the three sentences from Leslie's transcript you have chosen to analyze.

Sample:

Leslie 2   She gets her ingredients together and cracks some eggs into a

large bowl.

I assumed that she was using a cake mix and visualized a cake mix box. The speaker's use of "ingredients" was not necessarily misleading, but was not specific enough to show that the woman was making a cake from scratch.

Use this space for your analysis of Leslie's responses:

1. ____

____

2. ____

____

3. ____

____

Use this space for your analysis of Diana's responses:

1. ____

____

2. ____

____

3. ____

____

Leslie's responses tended to have a different form than Diana's. Did the form of Leslie's responses affect the visualizations that you created in response to Diana's sentences? Describe three examples where this happened.

1. ____

____

2. ____

____

3. ____

____

Step 4   Assessment

Select three of the six illustrations that you analyzed in step 3. Take the descriptions of successes or failures in conveying meaning from step 3 and discuss the role that visualization played in the success or failure in understanding the meaning as expressed by the speaker and the illustrations. A failure means that meaning was lost. This would mean that you envisioned a picture that was substantially different from the illustration shown in the workbook. Remember that your visualizations are based on what you hear and that what you hear is based on what that speaker understood from the illustration. Each speaker provides you with a different form to listen to. Differences in form that can affect meaning include omissions, additions, and a different perspective or view of what is conveyed in the illustration. Look for examples where information that was present in the illustration was not present in the spoken version and where information that was not present in the illustration was conveyed in the spoken version.

1.
____

____

2.
____

____

3.
____

____

Step 5　Action

Develop a plan for action based on your analysis and assessment of your understanding of the importance of visualizing and the difference between form and meaning. For example, select another illustration from this unit and go through the five-step follow-up again to improve your understanding of the difference between form and meaning. You can repeat this action step until you have worked carefully with each of the eight illustrations to fully understand the role of visualization and the difference between form and meaning.

____

____

____

____

____

EXERCISE 2.3

The Wading Pool

Please see Exercise 2.1 for instructions for the teacher.

Directions

Student Workbook
page 76

This selection is approximately three minutes long. Listen to and watch the video selection, answer the study questions, and then do the follow-up. You will need three different colored pens or pencils for this exercise, red, blue, and black. You will use these to mark differences that you find between your visualizations, the illustrations, and the transcripts. Each of the speaker's responses is numbered for easy reference. For example, Diana's first response is Diana 1, and Leslie's first response is Leslie 1.

Create Your Visualizations

Find this selection on your videotape. Do not look at the printed illustrations yet. Listen to Leslie describe each of the eight illustrations in the sequence. Visualize the images she is describing. Create a mental visualization or draw a quick sketch that represents what you heard her say. Keep track of the spatial relationships between the actors and objects she describes. Do not worry about your artistic ability, simply make a quick line drawing. Stick figures are fine. Do not write or say any English words to help you remember what she said. Stop the tape after each sentence when you hear the beep to give yourself enough time to create your visualization. Then, listen to Diana describe the same set of eight illustrations. Visualize or draw a quick sketch representing what you heard her say. Keep track of the spatial relationships between the actors and objects she describes. Do not use written or spoken English to help you remember what she said. You may draw while listening. Stop the tape at the end of the selection.

Visualizations Based on Leslie's Responses

1	2
3	4
5	6
7	8

Visualizations Based on Diana's Responses

1	2
3	4
5	6
7	8

Study Questions

1. Compare your visualizations or drawings created in response to Leslie's sentences with the illustrations on page 81 (Teacher's Guide page 98). Look at each of the illustrations. In each illustration circle in blue any differences between your visualization and the illustrations. The differences might be due to information that is either missing or added by the speaker or to information that you assumed was included, but was not. For each of the eight illustrations decide if the meaning of your visualization is the same or different from the illustration. Write "same" or "different" in the corresponding numbered spaces below.

   1. _______________________________

   2. _______________________________

   3. _______________________________

   4. _______________________________

   5. _______________________________

   6. _______________________________

   7. _______________________________

   8. _______________________________

2. Compare your visualizations or drawings created in response to Diana's sentences with the illustrations on page 81 (Teacher's Guide page 98). Look at each of the illustrations. In each illustration circle in red any differences between your visualization and the illustration. The differences might be due to information that is either missing or added by the speaker or to information that you assumed was included, but was not. For each of the eight illustrations decide if the meaning of your visualization is the same or different from the illustration and write "same" or "different" in the numbered spaces below.

1. _______________________________

2. _______________________________

3. _______________________________

4. _______________________________

5. _______________________________

6. _______________________________

7. _______________________________

8. _______________________________

3. Using your answers to question 1, select the illustrations that you have marked as being different in meaning from your visualization. For each of these differences, refer to the transcript of Leslie's spoken English and determine which part of the utterance led you to create a visualization that differed in meaning from the original illustration and underline it in black.

4. Using your answers to question 2, select the illustrations that you have marked as being different in meaning from your visualization. For each of these differences, refer to the transcript of Diana's spoken English and determine which part of the utterance led you to create a visualization that differed in meaning from the original illustration and underline it in black.

5. Read the transcript of Leslie's responses and compare it to the illustration it describes. Underline in blue any information in the transcript that is not in the illustration. Your visualization is based on what you heard and should contain the same additions.

6. Read the transcript of Diana's responses and compare it to the illustration it describes. Underline in red any information in the transcript that is not in the illustration or your visualization. Your visualization is based on what you heard and should contain the same additions.

Transcript *The Wading Pool*

Leslie's responses to illustrations of the wading pool:

Leslie 1   There is a little boy pumping up his inflatable pool while his dog stands by.

Leslie 2   The pool is filled up with air and then he gets a hose and puts water in the pool. The dog is still waiting.

Leslie 3   Next we see the hose flying out of the boy's hand and the dog is going headlong into the pool.

Leslie 4   The dog doesn't like it much when the boy squirts him with the hose.

Leslie 5   Even though the dog has jumped out of the pool the boy is still after him with that hose.

Leslie 6   The boy is sitting alone in the pool, with his boat. Unbeknownst to him the dog is sitting nearby waiting to get into some mischief.

Leslie 7   That clever little dog takes a nip of the pool and takes out all of the air, the water too.

Leslie 8   Now the boy is sitting in his deflated pool with no water and the dog is nearby, wagging his tail.

Diana's responses to illustrations of the wading pool:

Diana 1   A boy inflates his swimming pool while his dog looks on.

Diana 2   The little boy happily pours water into his swimming pool.

Diana 3   And then the dog jumps into the filled up swimming pool.

Diana 4   The boy squirts water on the dog.

Diana 5   The dog runs away.

Diana 6	The boy happily plays in the swimming pool, while the dog sneaks up behind him.
Diana 7	The dog chomps on the swimming pool, causing the pool to deflate.
Diana 8	The boy sits in the deflated swimming pool, while the dog chews on part of the pool.

Five-Step Follow-up

Step 1   Observation

Review your responses to all parts of the exercise that you have done so far. Make sure all parts are complete.

Step 2   Selection

Refer to your answers to study questions 3 and 4. These are the places where you noted that your visualization did not match the illustration itself. You have already underlined the portions of the transcript of Leslie's responses that may have led you to a different meaning than that shown in the illustration. Select three sentences from each speaker's transcript.

Step 3   Analysis

Explain how the underlined sections of the transcript affected your understanding of the meaning.

Use this space for your analysis of Leslie's responses:

1. ____

____

2. ____

____

3. ____

____

Use this space for your analysis of Diana's responses:

1. ____

____

2. ____

____

3. ____

____

In general, Leslie's responses tended to have a different form than Diana's. Did the form of Leslie's responses affect the visualizations that you created in response to Diana's sentences? Describe three examples where this happened.

1. ____

____

2. ____

____

3. ____

____

Step 4   Assessment

Assess your understanding of the difference between form and meaning. Select three of the six illustrations that you analyzed in step 3. Take the descriptions of successes or failures in conveying meaning from step 3 and discuss the role that visualization played in the success or failure in understanding the meaning as expressed by the speaker and the illustrations. A failure means that meaning was lost. This would mean that you envisioned a picture that was substantially different from the illustration shown in the workbook. Remember that your visualizations are based on what you hear and that what you hear is based on what that speaker understood from the illustration. Each speaker provides you with a different form to listen to. Differences in form that can affect meaning include omissions, additions, and a different perspective or view of what is conveyed in the illustration. Look for examples where information that was present in the illustration was not present in the spoken version and where information that was not present in the illustration was conveyed in the spoken version.

1. ____

____

2. ____

____

3. ____

____

Step 5   Action

Develop a plan for action based on your analysis and assessment of your understanding of the importance of visualizing and the difference between form and meaning. For example, select another illustration from this unit and go through the five-step follow-up again to improve your understanding of the difference between form and meaning. You can repeat this action step until you have worked carefully with each of the eight illustrations to fully understand the role of visualization and the difference between form and meaning.

____

____

____

____

____

____

____

____

Additional Exercises in Form and Meaning: Implicit and Explicit Information

Implicit information is information that is present but is not stated overtly. In some cases what is explicit in one language can be implicit in another. Sometimes the verbal description that you heard may have left out some information that you feel should be made explicit based on what is actually presented in the printed illustration.

1. Select one scenario from the three in this unit and examine the transcripts to determine if the spoken English conveyed all of the explicit information that was needed. Select specific utterances and rewrite them so that the explicit information is included.

____

____

____

____

____

____

2. How much implicit information is provided by the title? How does the title influence your perception of the content?

____

____

____

____

Progress Tracking Sheet

This sheet is designed to help you keep track of which exercises you have completed and how well you have done on these exercises. See page 13 (Teacher's Guide page 20) for a full description of how to use the Progress Tracking Sheet.

Exercise Number	Date	First Performance	Study Questions	Follow-up Activity	Questions and Reminders	Date	Second Performance
Exercise 2.1 Quantitative							
Qualitative							
Exercise 2.2 Quantitative							
Qualitative							
Exercise 2.3 Quantitative							
Qualitative							
Quantitative Totals							

Lexical Substitution

Introduction

Lexical substitution is the process of replacing a word or lexical item with another word or lexical item without changing the meaning of the message. In some cases a single word can be replaced by a phrase when the phrase functions as a unit, like an idiom, as long as the meaning is not changed. To create effective lexical substitutions students must master several important kinds of exercises at the word level. This unit provides exercises for five areas related to the word level of discourse. The five types are words as propositional units, specific and general words, primary and secondary meaning of words, collocations, and jargon.

Words as Propositional Units

A proposition is an idea unit. For example, the word "man" conveys several propositions or larger concepts such as adult, male, and mammal. This concept helps us realize that even within one word there can be many meanings or even a whole proposition. Larson (1984) refers to this concept as "unpacking." This is a good way to think of how to find the meaning within each word. For example, in the word "father" there are several concepts. We can unpack them as follows. The concepts within "father" can include human, adult, male, a person who has fathered a child, and possibly a person who is in a religious order who is not necessarily a biological father. When practicing lexical substitution, it is helpful to realize that a single word can include several propositions. Keep these propositions in mind as you search for other words that can substitute for the words in the exercise.

Specific Words to General Words

Some words are general in nature, such as collective nouns like "furniture." Other words are more specific, such as "sofa" or "love seat." Both the general and the specific words refer to something that you can sit on and that could be found in a living room. You can readily see that within the general term of furniture there are many more specific types of furniture that can be named. The technique of substituting a general word for a more specific word or vice versa is helpful for interpreters.

It is useful to develop lexical substitution skills because there will be times during the interpretation process when the exact word in the target language does not come to mind. When that happens, using a more general term can preserve the meaning and allow the interpretation to continue. Lexical substitution is important in translation and interpretation for another reason. Since words in the source language do not necessarily have a one-to-one correspondence with words in various target languages it is important to be able to select the word in the target language that comes closest in meaning to the word used in the source language.

Primary and Secondary Meaning

Many words have more than one meaning. After distinguishing form from meaning, the interpreter must determine which meaning is the most appropriate for the given context. The primary meaning is usually the first one listed in the dictionary, the most generic, or the first one that comes to mind for most people most of the time, in a given location. The linguistic and social context provides the most helpful way to determine which meaning is intended. When the interpreter has a large vocabulary and is able to analyze the linguistic and social context in which they find themselves, the interpreter is more likely to render an interpretation that is faithful to the intended message. The linguistic context includes information such as a speech or conversation. The social context is made up of the setting, such as a formal meeting or a hospital setting, and the people who are in the communicative event.

The secondary meaning is the one that usually occurs second in the dictionary or later. It is the meaning that comes to mind a bit later on, not the first thing that comes to mind for most people in a given location. Certain contexts may cause the secondary meaning to be the obvious choice. For example, if all the members of a class use a word in the same way in relation to their topic of study, it could easily be the secondary meaning rather than the primary meaning. For example, if the class members named themselves "The Lemmings" the word "lemmings" now refers to a group of students, not the group of animals known as lemmings.

Compounds and Collocations

Compounds are made up of two words that function as one word, but the meaning expressed by the compound is not always available by looking at the two words that comprise it. For example, the word blackboard is a compound and can be used to refer to a green board or even a white board, usually found in a classroom.

Collocations are constructions that contain two or more words that routinely occur in close proximity and function as a unit. Larson (1984, p. 141) writes, "Collocation is concerned with how words go together, i.e., which words may occur in constructions with which other words." She stresses that knowledge of collocations will help you know which words can sometimes be used together or never used together. She goes on to say that when people learn a second language they may make mistakes because they collocate words that may go together well in their native language but do not make sense next to each other in the second language. According to Baker (1992, p. 47), "Another way of looking at collocation would be to think of it in terms of the tendency of certain words to co-occur regularly in a given language." Some examples of collocations given by Baker include pay a visit, break rules, and wasting time. For a more detailed explanation of the various forms and functions of collocations see Baker (1992).

Jargon

Jargon is a kind of terminology that is used in a specific field or topic area. For example, in the field of computer science, there are many words that have meaning in that context that would be misunderstood in another context. Some examples are words like bit and bus. These words have specific meanings within the context of computer science and would have different meanings in other contexts. Jargon is special vocabulary that is used by people within a profession or group. Jargon has meaning for those people in the group and may be misunderstood or not understood by people who are not members of that group.

The Role of Lexical Substitution in the Interpretation Process

Developing lexical substitution skills increases linguistic flexibility. The ability to quickly find a synonym is one of the component skills required in the simultaneous interpretation process. Having a large vocabulary at your command can enhance your real world skills in simultaneous interpreting. The more words you have to express a specific concept, the better.

If you realize that a single word can contain an entire concept, it will be easier for you to correctly interpret. For example, if you know that the term "mother" has several concepts within it you will be better able to understand the term itself and to find acceptable lexical expressions in the target language. Another example of how lexical substitution skills can improve linguistic flexibility in the interpretation process is that in the event that the desired lexical item cannot be retrieved from memory, a description of what that word means might suffice.

In some cases it will be necessary to express the concept in a more formal way or in a more informal way than it was expressed in the original concept. These kinds of changes are called changes in register and can often be accomplished by lexical substitution. For example, the source language may be "The man gave a talk." If the target language had no equivalents in this fairly informal register, it might be necessary to say "The professor gave a lecture." In this case the higher register words are also more specific than the words used in the original.

In still other instances, there will be a collocation in the source language that can be expressed as a single word in the target language and vice versa. For example, the English collocations "spic and span" and "black and blue" may not be expressed in three words in another language, but perhaps in a single word like "clean" or "bruised." A thorough grounding in both the source and the target language will ensure correct usage and interpretation of collocations.

Jargon or special terminology may occur in the source language and not have a lexical equivalent in the target language, and so the jargon must be correctly understood and an appropriate term in the target language selected to convey the meaning. For example, if the topic is stained glass the following words may be used in a lecture: fid, flux, and came. You need to know what these terms mean in the context of stained glass in order to be able to interpret them correctly. If you can convey that the fid is the tool used to smooth the edges of the copper foil, the flux is the name of the acid that is put on top of the copper foil, and the came is the lead that is used to encase the edges of the glass, then the interpretation can convey the meaning of the original message. Jargon cannot be interpreted unless its meaning is understood in the source language. In situations where jargon is used you must take the time to familiarize yourself with the meaning and spelling of the words in order to be able to effectively interpret them.

Lexical substitution is one way to increase linguistic flexibility. In order to have rapid and effective lexical substitution skills you must have the ability to use words as propositional units, move from general to specific words or specific to general words, know register variation, and be aware of primary and secondary meanings of words. In addition, you must be able to use collocations correctly and deal appropriately with jargon.

Discussion Questions

Discuss the following questions with your students to promote interaction and increase awareness of the importance of lexical substitution skills as they relate to the interpretation process.

1. *How does an understanding of the lexical substitution process in English relate to the interpretation process?*

   Lexical substitution drills can increase the range of lexical items quickly available for the interpreter to use. Since the simultaneous interpretation process is so cognitively demanding, it is important to reduce cognitive effort wherever possible. One way to help reduce the effort needed is to practice the many tasks that make up the interpretation process. One of the relevant skills is lexical substitution. You can think of it as a high-speed synonym-finding drill. Be sure to point out that it is necessary to practice this skill within each of the languages in the interpretation process. Some students may feel that if English is their first language they do not need to study English during their interpretation studies. However, most students have not had the opportunity to practice English substitution drills. This skill can provide great linguistic flexibility for the interpreter.

2. *Do you feel you have good lexical substitution skills?*

   Ask this question before and after the drills and see if students feel their skills have improved and if they have greater confidence in them. Most students will improve with increased focus and practice. Confidence in the ability to find the necessary words quickly is beneficial to the interpreter. Rapid and reliable lexical substitution drills are not automatic. These skills must be learned and practiced. This question is designed to improve awareness of level before and after the exercises.

3. *What will happen if the interpreter does not have rapid, reliable lexical substitution skills?*

   When the interpreter does not have quick access to various ways to express the same concept, then the richness of the product is compromised. For example, if an interpreter is working from ASL to English and knows only one translation of a particular sign, the interpreter's work into English will be limited in scope and register. Register variation skills will allow the interpreter to provide an interpretation that matches the register requirements of the interpretation assignment.

4. *What happens when the interpreter does not know the meaning of the word that must be substituted?*

   If the interpreter does not understand the word, then they cannot find an appropriate substitute. This weakness indicates a need for greater vocabulary development.

Lexical Substitution Exercises

This unit has two types of lexical substitution exercises. The first is workbook-based which means that you can read and respond without the time pressure associated with responding to videotape. You do the workbook exercises in the workbook and work at your own pace. The second type of exercise is real-time. In the real-time exercises, you will be working from videotape, but you will stop the tape to provide your answers. Real-time practice has more time constraints than workbook, but not as much as simultaneous interpreting. For real-time exercises, you respond in spoken English immediately after you hear a sentence in English. This kind of workbook and then real-time practice is a developmental step toward mastering simultaneous interpretation skills.

WORKBOOK EXERCISE 3.1

Lexical Substitution

Begin this exercise by having a brief review discussion to be sure that students understand the concept of general and specific words. After the discussion, have the students fill in the exercise below, which goes from general to specific. This exercise can be done in a group or you can assign it for homework. Some suggested answers are provided, although you will find other answers acceptable. You could conduct a follow-up drill going from specific to more general words.

Decide if you want to conduct this exercise in class, or if you want the students to do this exercise on their own time. In either case, each student must have his or her own workbook. The exercises in this unit can be done in a group setting. Students respond by writing answers in the workbook.

Read the directions and explain them to the students. Allow time for questions after you have given the directions. You should plan on at least five minutes to prepare the students for the exercise. Five minutes should be enough, if you have the group's attention, and if all students have their workbooks ready.

Directions

Student Workbook
page 93

Below is a list of words. In the space provided, write as many words as you can that are more specific than the word in the left column. All of your answers must be semantically related to the word in the left-hand column.

Computer	_Mac, PC, Gateway, Compaq_
Dwelling	_house, townhouse, apartment, cave_
Animal	_dog, cat, lion, horse, zebra_
Clothing	_dress, suit, shorts, coat_
Timepiece	_clock, watch, grandfather clock_
Plant	_azalea, daisy, tree, bush_
Vehicle	_car, SUV, station wagon, truck_
Vegetable	_carrot, potato, corn, celery_
Tool	_hammer, saw, drill, hoe_
Ambulate	_walk, saunter, run, stroll_

WORKBOOK EXERCISE 3.2

Lexical Substitution

Directions

Student Workbook page 94

Substitute the underlined words in this story with another word or words. In some cases you can use more than one word. Be sure that the word you use as a replacement does not change the meaning of the underlined word.

Students may use a thesaurus if necessary to complete this exercise.

Gene's Trip to Canada

1   Last year, Gene took a <u>trip</u> _________ _vacation_ _________ to Canada.

2   He left early in July and was gone for two <u>months</u>

3   _________ _eight weeks_ _________. He decided to <u>travel</u>

4   _________ _go_ _________ by train so that he could see

5   more <u>scenery</u> _________ _vistas, of the country_ _________ and <u>relax</u>

6   _________ _enjoy it, unwind_ _________. He bought his ticket several

7   months in <u>advance</u> _________ _early_ _________. When it

8   was time to <u>board</u> _______________ *get on* _______________ the

9   train he was really <u>happy</u> _________ *glad, delighted* _________

10   and relieved that the time had come for his <u>vacation</u>

11   _____________ *trip, adventure* _____________ to begin.

12   His destination was the Canadian Rockies, where he planned to

13   visit Banff and see the <u>area</u> _________ *vicinity, sights* _________

14   around that town. When he finally reached the Rockies he got off the

15   train. He rented a <u>small</u> _________ *compact, economy* _________ car and

16   looked for a hotel to stay in. He wanted to stay in a hotel in Banff, but

17   found that it was too <u>expensive</u> _________ *costly, pricey* _________ .

18   He stayed at a motel instead.

19   He traveled around the area for several days. He was most

20   <u>impressed</u> _________ *struck by, thrilled* _________ with the glaciers.

21   Eventually he had to return home. He left with many beautiful

22   memories and <u>photos</u> _________ *snapshots, pictures* _________ .

The rest of the workbook lexical substitution exercises are the transcripts from Diana and Leslie's responses to a set of pictures. Later you will work with the same material on the video in its spoken English form.

WORKBOOK EXERCISE 3.3

Opening a Can

Directions

Student Workbook
page 95

Replace the underlined words with a word or two that means the same thing as the underlined word. Diana and Leslie were both looking at the same pictures and provided these spoken English sentences in response to those pictures. Their spoken English is transcribed.

First do this exercise in the workbook. Using the printed materials, take a few minutes to discuss possible and logical answers. Then move to the real-time version of this exercise. The workbook version gives the students a chance to practice "unpacking" and can result in a better understanding of the words that are underlined. This unpacking strategy can provide a good starting place for a translation.

Diana's response to Opening a Can:

Diana 1   A <u>man</u> _________ *adult male, guy* _________ has a can and a can opener.

Diana 2   He uses the <u>can opener</u> _____ *device for opening cans, utensil* _____ to begin taking the lid off the can.

Diana 3   The man puts down the can opener and takes the <u>lid</u> _________________ *top* _________________ off the can.

Leslie's response to Opening a Can:

Leslie 1   There is a man getting ready to open a <u>can</u> _________________ *container* _________________ of tomatoes. A can opener is lying on the counter.

Leslie 2   Next we see him opening the can with that <u>manual</u> _________ *hand-operated* _________ can opener.

Leslie 3   Finally he removes the lid and the can opener is back on the <u>counter</u> _________ *table* _________ .

Study Questions

1. Write the words that you have selected to replace the underlined words in Diana's responses. After each answer, indicate if your response is a more general or more specific word than the original word. If it is a synonym it may be neither more nor less specific.

Diana 1

____

____

Diana 2

____

____

Diana 3

____

____

2. Write the words that you have selected to replace the underlined words in Leslie's responses. After each answer, indicate if your response is a more general or more specific word than the original word. If it is a synonym it may be neither more nor less specific.

Leslie 1

____

____

Leslie 2

____

____

Leslie 3

____

____

3. Study each of Diana's responses. Unpack as many nouns as you can without changing the meaning. Then replace as many verbs as you can without changing the meaning. Write those replacement words in the space provided.

Some nouns and verbs are listed here as examples. Others may be acceptable.

Nouns

Man—adult male

Can—metal container

Can opener—device for opening cans

Lid—top, end of can

Verbs

Has—possesses

Uses—employs

To begin—to start

Taking off—removing

4. Study each of Leslie's responses. Unpack as many nouns as you can without changing the meaning. Then replace as many verbs as you can without changing the meaning. Write those replacement words in the space provided. If you have already unpacked some of the nouns and verbs that Leslie uses, you do not need to do them again.

Nouns

Tomatoes—large, edible berry, red or yellow

Counter—board or table

Manual—hand-operated

Verbs

Is—exists. It is unlikely that students will choose to replace "is."

See—perceive with the eyes

Removes—takes or moves away

5. Write down any compounds or collocations that occurred in either Diana's or Leslie's responses.

There are no true compounds or collocations.

____

Five-Step Follow-up

Step 1   Observation

Check all of your answers to be sure they are complete.

Step 2   Selection

Select your answers to study questions 1 and 2. These are the words you chose as lexical substitutes for the underlined words. Make a list of any of your answers that are not equivalent in meaning to the original word. You will know which ones are not equivalent based on the dictionary definitions of the words.

____

____

____

____

____

____

Step 3   Analysis

Use a thesaurus to find synonyms for all of the underlined words in the original text. What percentage of the words that you used as replacement words are acceptable substitutes according to the dictionary? Divide the number of right answers by the total number of words to be replaced to get the percentage. Write that percentage here.

____

It is unusual to attach a percentage to specific aspects of interpreter training exercises because there are so many variables in each message. However, this system of deriving a percentage can allow students to get a feel for how they are doing. It should be stressed that in most instances, percentages are not usually relevant be-cause interpretations are not judged "right" or "wrong." This is simply a training technique and should be explained as such to students.

Scores from 86 to 100% are considered good.

Scores from 75 to 85% are considered fair.

Scores below 75% indicate below-average work.

Step 4   **Assessment**

Look at the percentage that you derived in step 3. Is it close to 100? If not, then this tells you that you need to spend more time studying the definitions of words and finding words that are synonyms.

Step 5   **Action**

Create vocabulary cards that you can carry with you. When you hear a word whose meaning you are not sure of, write that word down, look it up as soon as possible, and write the definition on the same card. Try to use that word in conversation twice in the same week that you looked it up in the dictionary.

Using cards or other portable reminders of new words is an effective way to improve vocabulary.

WORKBOOK EXERCISE 3.4

Climbing a Stepladder

Directions

Student Workbook page 99

Substitute the underlined words in this story with another word. In some cases you can use more than one word. Be sure that the word you use as a replacement does not change the meaning of the underlined word.

Students may use a thesaurus if necessary to complete this exercise.

Diana's responses to Climbing a Stepladder:

Diana 1   A <u>woman</u> _________ *adult female, lady* _________ begins to step

on a stepladder.

Diana 2   She <u>climbs</u> _________ *goes up* _________ to the second step of the stepladder.

Diana 3   Now <u>she</u> _________ *the lady, the woman* _________ is at the top of the stepladder.

Leslie's responses to Climbing a Stepladder:

Leslie 1   There is a <u>young girl</u> _________ *child, kid* _________ making her way up a stepstool. There are two steps in all and she is on the first step.

Leslie 2   Now she is on the second <u>step</u>, _________ *rung, level* _________ crouched over on her way to the top.

Leslie 3   Now she is <u>standing</u> _________ *upright* _________ on the very top step.

Study Questions

1. Write the words that you have selected to replace the underlined words in Diana's responses. After each answer, indicate if your response is a more general or more specific word than the original word.

Diana 1   ____

____

Diana 2   ____

____

Diana 3   ____

____

2. Write the words that you selected to replace the underlined words in Leslie's responses. After each answer, indicate if your response is a more general or more specific word than the original word.

Leslie 1

____

____

Leslie 2

____

____

Leslie 3

____

____

3. Study each of Diana's responses. Replace as many nouns as you can without changing the meaning. Then replace as many verbs as you can without changing the meaning. Write those replacement words in the space provided.

Nouns

____

____

____

____

Verbs

____

____

____

4. Study each of Leslie's responses. Replace as many nouns as you can without changing the meaning. Then replace as many verbs as you can without changing the meaning. Write those replacement words in the space provided.

Nouns

____

____

____

____

Verbs

____

____

____

____

5. Write down any compounds or collocations that occurred in either
    Diana's or Leslie's responses.

    ____

    ____

    ____

    ____

Five-Step Follow-up

Step 1   Observation

Check all of your answers to be sure they are complete.

Step 2   Selection

Select your answers to study questions 1 and 2. These are the words you have
chosen as lexical substitutes for the underlined words. Make a list of any of
your answers that are not equivalent in meaning to the original word. You
will know which ones are not equivalent based on the dictionary definitions
of the words.

____

____

____

____

____

____

Step 3   Analysis

Use a thesaurus to find synonyms for all of the underlined words in the original text. What percentage of the words that you used, as replacement words were acceptable substitutes according to the dictionary? Divide the number of right answers by the total number of words replaced to get the percentage. Write that percentage here.

____

Step 4   Assessment

Look at the percentage that you derived in step 3. Is it close to 100? If not, then this tells you that you need to spend more time studying the definitions of words and finding words that are synonyms.

Step 5   Action

Create vocabulary cards that you can carry with you. When you hear a word whose meaning you are not sure of, write that word down, look it up as soon as possible, and write the definition on the same card. Use that word in conversation twice in the same week that you looked it up in the dictionary.

WORKBOOK EXERCISE 3.5

Grooming the Dog

Directions

Student Workbook page 104

Substitute the underlined words in this story with another word. In some cases you can use more than one word. Be sure that the word you use as a replacement does not change the meaning of the underlined word.

Students may use a thesaurus if necessary to complete this exercise.

Diana's responses to Grooming the Dog:

Diana 1   A man is <u>petting</u> _________ *patting, stroking* _________ his dog.

Diana 2   Now he is <u>brushing</u> _________ *grooming* _________ his dog.

Diana 3   Now the man is <u>kneeling</u>, _________ *on his knees* _________ looking at his dog.

Leslie's responses to Grooming the Dog:

Leslie. 1   There is a man and his dog who looks like he has just been <u>bathed</u> _________ *washed* _________ .

Leslie. 2   Now we see the man brushing the dog's <u>coat</u> _________ *fur* _________ .

Leslie 3   Next we see the dog sitting down and the man looking <u>proudly</u> _________ *with pride,* _________ at his well-groomed pet.

Study Questions

1. Write the words that you selected to replace the underlined words in Diana's responses. After each answer, indicate if your response is a more general or more specific word than the original word.

Diana 1 ____

____

Diana 2 ____

____

Diana 3 ____

____

2. Write the words that you selected to replace the underlined words in Leslie's responses. After each answer, indicate if your response is a more general or more specific word than the original word.

Leslie 1 ____

____

Leslie 2 ____

____

Leslie 3 ____

____

3. Study each of Diana's responses. Replace as many nouns as you can without changing the meaning. Then replace as many verbs as you can without changing the meaning. Write those replacement words in the space provided.

Nouns

____

____

____

____

____

Verbs

____

____

____

____

4. Study each of Leslie's responses. Replace as many nouns as you can without changing the meaning. Then replace as many verbs as you can without changing the meaning. Write those replacement words in the space provided.

Nouns

____

____

____

____

Verbs

____

____

____

____

5. Write down any compounds or collocations that occurred in either Diana's or Leslie's responses.

____

____

____

____

Five-Step Follow-up

Step 1   Observation

Check all of your answers to be sure they are complete.

Step 2   Selection

Select your answers to study questions 1 and 2. These are the words you have chosen as lexical substitutes for the underlined words. Make a list of any of your answers that are not equivalent in meaning to the original word. You will know which ones are not equivalent based on the dictionary definitions of the words.

____

____

____

____

____

Step 3   Analysis

Use a thesaurus to find synonyms for all of the underlined words in the original text. What percentage of the words that you used as replacement words are acceptable substitutes according to the dictionary? Divide the number of right answers by the total number of words to be replaced to get the percentage. Write that percentage here.

____

Step 4   Assessment

Look at the percentage that you derived in step 3. Is it close to 100? If not, then this tells you that you need to spend more time studying the definitions of words and finding words that are synonyms.

Step 5   Action

Create vocabulary cards that you can carry with you. When you hear a word whose meaning you are not sure of, write that word down, look it up as soon as possible, and write the definition on the same card. Try to use that word in conversation twice in the same week that you looked it up in the dictionary.

REAL-TIME EXERCISE 3.1

Opening a Can

This exercise uses the same sentences that were used in the workbook version of the exercise. Using the same sentences means that the students will already know the answers. The point of this exercise is to get the feeling of quickly substituting one word for another in real-time when the answer is already familiar to the student. Refer to the workbook version for possible answers. Time is provided between sentences on the video. If this is not enough time to respond, students may stop the tape and then respond. There are no study questions and no follow-up for Real-Time Exercises 3.1 through 3.3. Instead, students are asked to write a statement about their ability to do substitution in real-time. Real-Time Exercises 3.4 and 3.5 do have study questions and follow-up exercises.

Decide if you want to conduct this exercise in class, or if you want the students to do this exercise on their own time. If students do this exercise on their own time, each student must have his or her own source tape and workbook. This exercise can be done in a group setting only if each student has a way to record his or her spoken English responses without auditory interference. Individual stations in a language lab is the recommended arrangement. If a language lab or similar arrangement is not available, then students should do these exercises out of class.

Whether the students do the exercises in class or on their own time, it is good to spend time going over the directions as a group. Read the directions and explain them to the students. Allow time for questions after you have given the directions. You should plan on at least five minutes to prepare the students for the exercise. Five minutes should be enough, if you have the group's attention, and if all equipment is ready and in working order. All tapes needed for this exercise must be cued to the correct spot. This includes the source tape and any tapes that will be used for recording.

Directions

Student Workbook
page 108

This selection is about two minutes long. Make your recording. You will need your tape recorder and a blank tape for this exercise. Diana and Leslie were both looking at the same pictures and provided these spoken English sentences in response to those pictures. The transcripts of their spoken English are printed below.

Find this selection on your video. This selection is about two minutes long. Press "record" on your tape recorder and then press "play" on your VCR. Listen to Diana's first sentence and stop the videotape when you hear the beep, leaving the tape recorder running. Repeat the entire sentence using the replacement word that you used for the workbook version of this exercise. You may follow along by reading from the printed version of transcripts that you used in the workbook version. Each of the speaker's responses is numbered for easy reference. For example, Diana's first response is Diana 1 and Leslie's first response is Leslie 1.

See suggested answers in the workbook version.

Transcript for *Opening a Can*

Diana's responses to Opening a Can:

Diana 1   A <u>man</u> _________________________________ has a can and a

can opener.

Diana 2   He uses the <u>can opener</u> _______________________________

to begin taking the lid off the can.

Diana 3   The man puts down the can opener and takes the <u>lid</u>

_________________________________ off the can.

Leslie's responses to Opening a Can:

Leslie 1   There is a man getting ready to open a <u>can</u>

_________________________________ of tomatoes. A can opener

is lying on the counter.

Leslie 2   Next we see him opening the can with that <u>manual</u>

_________________________________ can opener.

Leslie. 3   Finally he removes the lid and the can opener is back on the

<u>counter</u> ___________________________________.

Write a statement that describes your reaction to your performance in Real-Time Exercise 3.1. Was it easy to do the substitution? Were you fluent-sounding? If it was difficult, say why.

____

____

____

____

REAL-TIME EXERCISE 3.2

Climbing a Stepladder

See Real-time Lexical Substitution Exercise 3.1 for instructions for the teacher.

Directions

Student Workbook
page 110

This selection is about two minutes long. Make your recording. You will need your tape recorder and a blank tape for this exercise. Diana and Leslie were both looking at the same pictures and provided these spoken English sentences in response to those pictures. The transcripts of their spoken English are printed below.

Set your videotape to the beginning of this selection. Press "record" on your tape recorder and then press "play" on your VCR. Listen to Diana's first sentence and stop the videotape, leaving the tape recorder running. Repeat the entire sentence using the replacement word that you used in the workbook version of this exercise. You may follow along by reading from the printed version of transcripts that you used in the workbook version of this exercise. Each of the speaker's responses is numbered for easy reference. For example, Diana's first response is Diana 1 and Leslie's first response is Leslie 1.

Transcript for *Climbing a Stepladder*

Diana's responses to Climbing a Stepladder:

Diana 1   A <u>woman</u> ____________________________________ begins to step on a stepladder.

Diana 2   She <u>climbs</u> ____________________________________ to the second step of the stepladder.

Diana 3   Now <u>she</u> ____________________________________ is at the top of the stepladder.

Leslie's responses to Climbing a Stepladder.

Leslie 1   There is a <u>young girl</u> ____________________________________ making her way up a stepstool. There are two steps in all and she is on the first step.

Leslie 2   Now she is on the second <u>step</u>, ____________________________________ crouched over on her way to the top.

Leslie 3   Now she is <u>standing</u> ____________________________________ on the very top step. If it was difficult, say why.

Write a statement that describes your reaction to your performance in Real-Time Exercise 3.1. Was it easy to do the substitution? Were you fluent-sounding? If it was difficult, say why.

____

____

____

____

REAL-TIME EXERCISE 3.3

Grooming the Dog

See Real-time Lexical Substitution Exercise 3.1 for instructions for the teacher.

Directions

Student Workbook
page 111

This selection is about two minutes long. Listen to it and make your recording. You will need your tape recorder and a blank tape for this exercise. Diana and Leslie were both looking at the same pictures and provided these spoken English sentences in response to those pictures. The transcripts of their spoken English are printed below.

Set your videotape to the beginning of this selection. Press "record" on your tape recorder and then press "play" on your VCR. Listen to Diana's first sentence and stop the videotape, leaving the tape recorder running. Repeat the entire sentence using the replacement word that you used in the workbook version of this exercise. You may follow along by reading from the printed version of transcripts that you used in the workbook version of this exercise. Each of the speaker's responses is numbered for easy reference. For example, Diana's first response is Diana 1 and Leslie's first response is Leslie 1.

Transcript for *Grooming the Dog*

Diana's responses to Grooming the Dog:

Diana 1   A man is <u>petting</u> _________________________ his dog.

Diana 2   Now he is <u>brushing</u> _________________________

his dog.

Diana 3   Now the man is <u>kneeling</u>, _________________________ looking

at his dog.

Leslie's responses to Grooming the Dog:

Leslie 1   There is a man and his dog who looks like he has just been

<u>bathed</u> _________________________.

Leslie 2   Now we see the man brushing the dog's <u>coat</u>

_______________________________.

Leslie 3   Next we see the dog sitting down and the man looking <u>proudly</u>

_______________________________ at his well-groomed pet.

Write a statement that describes your reaction to your performance in Real-Time Exercise 3.1. Was it easy to do the substitution? Were you fluent-sounding? If it was difficult, say why.

____

____

____

____

Spoken Material in Continuous Discourse

EXERCISE 3.4

How to Thread a Needle
BOBBI JORDAN

This exercise provides practice with lexical substitution in running discourse. The previous lexical substitution exercises have been at the sentence level only, so this one should be substantially more difficult. It is best to do this in workbook mode first but you can omit that step if you feel your students are ready to try this exercise in real-time mode. The selection has pauses in it so that the student has time to respond without stopping the tape. If more time is needed, the tape can be stopped or paused while the student responds.

Please see the directions to the teacher at the beginning of this unit for additional guidance.

Directions

This selection is approximately three minutes long. This exercise can be done both in the workbook and in real-time. After the substitution drill, answer the study questions and do the follow-up.

Workbook Lexical Substitution

First do the exercise in workbook mode by reading the transcript of "How to Thread a Needle." Replace each underlined word with another word that is equivalent in meaning. Do not change the meaning of the sentence or the overall meaning of the passage.

Transcript for *How to Thread a Needle,* by Bobbi Jordan

You can accept words that make sense in this context or you can require that students use synonyms. The italicized words are acceptable lexical substitutes.

1   Hi. My name is Bobbi Jordan, and today I'm going to teach you to

2   thread a needle. Now, I know what you're saying—that you already

3   know how to <u>thread a needle</u> 1.________________*do that*________________.

4   But, for very young eyes, or for very old eyes, threading a needle is

5   not an easy <u>thing</u> 2._________________*task*_________________ at all. And

6   sometimes even for people who have good sight it is <u>difficult</u>

7   3.___________*hard, not easy*___________, and so there's little tricks

8   along the way. As you can see, I don't have the best of eyes but I still

9   can thread the <u>tiniest</u> 4._________________*smallest*_________________

10 of needles.

11   Step 1: You need to hold the needle up so that it is against

12 something white or that light is passing through the eye of the

13 needle. If you try to thread a needle with a dark background

14 you can't see through it very well. So if you remember that you

15 need something light in back of it, you'll have an easier <u>chance</u>

16 5._________________*time*_________________ of getting the thread through.

17   Step 2: Thread is round. The eye of the needle is oblong. A lot of

18 times you'll get the thread right up to the needle, you'll know you're

19   right at the eye, and it will not go through. You can fix that <u>simply</u>

20   6._____________*easily*_____________ by biting the end of your

21   thread, just like that, so that it's flat. Now you have a flat object going

22   through an oblong object—ahh, yes. You pull the thread through—

23   while it's in there.

24   Step 3: Kids today—and I watch them because I make <u>costumes</u>

25   7._________*wardrobe, attire*_____________ —cannot do a rolled knot.

26   Your grannies could do it; Aunt Tillie could do it, but I <u>watch</u>

27   8._____________*observe*_____________ kids try to tie a knot like they

28   tie their shoes when there's a much easier way to do that. You take the

29   end of the thread, alright, and you moisten it—like that. Now you're

30   gonna wrap that thread around your index finger. When you first

31   start this, you want to wrap it a <u>LOT of</u> 9._____________*many*_____________

32   times, because the trick is then to roll your thumb over the thread,

33   and you will <u>make</u> 10.____________*have, tie*____________ a knot.

34   The knot comes out just as big as you want to make it.

35   This is about the size of the state of Texas, I see, but anyway,

36   you'll do better than that. I'm gonna <u>repeat</u> 11.____________*say*________

37   that again because I know a lot of you can't do that. You take your

38   index finger, you roll the thread around—when you're <u>rehearsing</u>

39   12.____________*practicing*____________ you can roll it around 7, 8,

40   9, 10 times and you have this big, fat wad. You push that thread with

41   your thumb off the end of that finger and then you pull it into a knot.

42   And so you have a good threaded needle, you have a nice knot, and

43   you're <u>ready</u> 13._______________*set*_______________ to sew on a

44   button. Can I repeat those steps for you? You need to remember <u>them</u>

45   14.____________*the steps*____________. First, you make <u>sure</u>

46   15._____________*certain*_____________ that you can see light or

47   white through the eye of the needle. <u>Second</u> 16._______*next*________,

48   you bite the thread so that it'll go through the needle easily; you pull

49   it through and down. Next, you wrap the end of your thread around

50   this index finger, and then you push that thread off, rolling it over

51   top, off of that—and pull it into a knot. Couldn't be <u>easier</u>

52   17.________________*simpler*________________ .

Real-Time Lexical Substitution

Find this selection on your tape and prepare your recording device to record your answers. Play the videotape and press "record" on your tape recorder. When you hear a beep tone on the videotape, replace the word that Bobbi said just prior to the beep. Choose a word that means the same thing as the original word. Stop the VCR at the end of this selection and then fill in the study questions.

Study Questions

1. Read the transcript and look at the words you wrote as replacement words for the first ten lines of "How to Thread a Needle." After each answer, indicate if it is a more general or more specific word than the original word. If it is neither, state that. State if you used unpacking to create your lexical substitution. Use a dictionary or thesaurus to see if your answers convey the same meaning as the original word.

   The lexical substitutes provided in lines 1–10 are neither more nor less specific than the original words.

2. Write the words that you selected to replace the underlined words in lines 11–20 of "How to Thread a Needle." After each answer, indicate if it is a more general or more specific word than the original word. If it is neither, state that. Use a dictionary or thesaurus to see if your answers convey the same meaning as the original word.

   The lexical substitutes in lines 11–20 are neither more nor less general than the original words with the following exception: "tie" is more specific than "do."

3. Write the words that you selected to replace the underlined words in lines 21–30 of "How to Thread a Needle." After each answer, indicate if it is a more general or more specific word than the original word. If it is neither, state that. Use a dictionary or thesaurus to see if your answers convey the same meaning as the original word.

   Most are neither, with the following exceptions: "tie" is more specific than "make."

4. Write the words that you selected to replace the underlined words in lines 31–52 of "How to Thread a Needle." After each answer, indicate if it is a more general or more specific word than the original word. If it is neither,

state that. Use a dictionary or thesaurus to see if your answers convey the same meaning as the original word.

"The steps" is more specific than "them" and "next" is less specific than "second."

5. List all the collocations you can find in "How to Thread a Needle."

The following could be considered collocations; thread a needle, eye of a

needle, index finger

List all the examples of figurative language you can find in "How to Thread a Needle."

big as the state of Texas

6. Listen to your recording of your real-time lexical substitutions. Write a statement that describes your work. Is it natural-sounding, and without hesitation?

Five-Step Follow-up

Step 1   Observation

Check all of your answers to be sure they are complete.

Step 2   Selection

Select your answers to study questions 1, 2, 3, and 4. These are the words you chose as lexical substitutes for the underlined words. Make a list of any of your answers that are not equivalent in meaning to the original word.

Here you would expect to see words that make sense in this context but are not equivalent in meaning to the original.

Step 3   **Analysis**

Use a thesaurus to find synonyms for all of the underlined words in the original text. What percentage of the words that you used as replacement words are acceptable substitutes according to the dictionary? Divide the number of right answers by the total number of words to be replaced to get the percentage. Write that percentage here.

See comment in previous exercise.

Step 4   **Assessment**

Look at the percentage that you derived in step 3. Is it close to 100? If not, then this tells you that you need to spend more time studying the definitions of words and finding words that are synonyms.

Step 5   **Action**

Redo the real-time exercise to get comfortable with lexical substitution.

EXERCISE 3.5

How to Order Fast Food
PETER LEARY

Please see directions to the teacher in Exercise 3.4. Although this is a familiar topic, the speaker uses some word choices that you would not expect to hear in this kind of description.

Directions

Student Workbook
page 118

This selection is approximately four minutes long. This exercise is done both as a workbook and a real-time exercise. After the substitution drill, answer the study questions and do the follow-up.

Workbook Lexical Substitution

First do the exercise in workbook mode by reading the transcript of "How to Order Fast Food." Replace each underlined word with another word that is equivalent in meaning. Do not change the meaning of the sentence or the overall meaning of the passage.

Transcript for *How to Order Fast Food,* by Peter Leary

The italicized words are words that are acceptable lexical substitutes. You can accept words that make sense in this context or you can require that students use synonyms.

1   Hello. I'm Peter Leary, and I'm gonna tell you how to order fast

2   food at a fast food restaurant. One of the most <u>paramount</u>

3   1.__________*important*__________ steps—crucial to the

4   whole process—is finding the fast food <u>establishment</u>

5   2.__________*place*__________ of your choice. If you don't go

6   through this <u>step</u> 3.__________*part*__________, you won't

7   go through any of the rest. Once you get there you have to be

8   <u>prepared</u> 4.__________*ready*__________. Fast food lists are

9   sometimes <u>voluminous</u> 5.__________*lengthy, long*__________ and

10   have many items. So, you sit back there, you start looking, and they

11   have all these different *things* 6.__________*items, choices*__________.

12   You can go (as the French would say) <u>a la carte</u> 7.__________*one item at*

13   *a time*__________, get a hamburger and fries, or you can go for the <u>infamous</u>

14   8.__________*notorious*__________ combination. Get a hamburger,

15   fries, a drink—small deduction in the <u>price</u> 9.__________*cost*__________.

16   So, you can read the menu now. Now it's <u>crucial</u> 10.__________*important*

17   to assess how hungry you are. If you're not hungry, maybe you

18   shouldn't be <u>eating</u> 11.________*consuming food*________. If you're

19   a little hungry, perhaps go for the small sizes. These are typically

20   <u>denoted</u> 12.__________*indicated*__________ by small letters

21   saying "small" on the menu; maybe medium—some restaurants like

22   to try and <u>trick</u> 13.____________*fool*____________ you. If

23   you're really hungry, go for large: they, ah, say large. So, you've gotten

24   past that part. But then you get to the hamburgers, quarter-pound,

25   third-pound, really hungry—what do I want? Hmm..., let me think.

26   <u>Least common denominators</u> 14.________*smallest divisor*________:

27   twelve. A quarter of a pound is actually $\frac{3}{12}$, third of a pound is $\frac{4}{12}$, I'm

28   hungry—I wanna get $\frac{4}{12}$—I'm gettin' the third of a pound hamburger.

29   Now you've <u>conquered</u> 15.__________*mastered*__________ one

30   of the harder selections. So you can go up to the cash register.

31   Remember: always be kind and <u>courteous</u> 16.______*polite*______.

32   These people are gonna give you your <u>food</u> 17.________*meal*________

33   so try to impress <u>them</u> 18.______*the people behind the counter*______.

34   And don't make them <u>angry</u> 19.__________*mad*__________.

35   Make your <u>selection</u> 20.__________*choices*__________, perhaps,

36   mmm, fries and a <u>drink</u> 21.__________*soda, beverage*__________,

37   they're gonna ask for some money, give them the <u>sum</u>

38   22.__________*amount*__________ of money they request, and

39   then wait a few <u>seconds</u> 23.__________*minutes*__________. In a few

40   seconds, you'll have your fast food. And that's what it is—few

41   seconds, fast food, and you know how to order it.

Real-Time Lexical Substitution

Find this selection on your tape and prepare your recording device to record your answers. Play the videotape and press "record" on your tape recorder. When you hear a beep tone on the videotape, replace the word that Peter said just prior to the beep. Choose a word that means the same thing as the original word. Stop the VCR at the end of this selection and then fill in the study questions.

Study Questions

1. Read the answers you wrote in the blanks in the workbook version of the exercise and write down the words you recorded as replacement words for the first 15 lines of "How to Order Fast Food." After each answer, indicate if it is a more general or more specific word than the original word. If it is neither, state that.

   The lexical substitutes have provided in lines 1–15 are neither more nor less specific than the original word.

2. Write the words that you selected to replace the underlined words in lines 16–30 of "How to Order Fast Food." After each answer, indicate if it is a more general or more specific word than the original word. If it is neither, state that.

   The lexical substitutes in lines 16–30 are neither more nor less general than the original words.

3. Write the words that you selected to replace the underlined words in lines 31–41 of "How to Order Fast Food." After each answer, indicate if it is a more general or more specific word than the original word. If it is neither, state that.

   Most are neither, with the following exceptions:

   Food—meal, meal is more specific

   Them—the people behind the counter is more specific

   Drink—soda is more specific, beverage is less specific.

4. List all the collocations you can find in "How to Order Fast Food."

   The following could be considered collocations: fast food, hamburger and fries, fries and a drink, cash register

5. List all the examples of jargon you can find in "How to Order Fast Food."

Quarter pounder, a la carte

6. Listen to your recording of your real-time lexical substitutions. Write a statement that describes your work. Is it natural-sounding, and without hesitation?

Five-Step Follow-up

Step 1   Observation

Check all of your answers to be sure they are complete.

Encourage students to review the study questions for completeness.

Step 2   Selection

Select your answers to study questions 1, 2, and 3. These are the words you chose as lexical substitutes for the underlined words. Make a list of any of your answers that are not equivalent in meaning to the original word.

Here you would expect to see words that make sense in this context but are not equivalent in meaning to the original.

Step 3   **Analysis**

Use a thesaurus to find synonyms for all of the underlined words in the original text. What percentage of the words that you used as replacement words are acceptable substitutes according to the dictionary? Divide the number of right answers by the total number of words to be replaced to get the percentage. Write that percentage here.

____

See comment in previous exercise.

Step 4   **Assessment**

Look at the percentage that you derived in step 3. Is it close to 100? If not, then this tells you that you need to spend more time studying the definitions of words and finding words that are synonyms.

Step 5   **Action**

Redo the real-time exercise to get comfortable with lexical substitution. Another action step is to create vocabulary cards that you can carry with you. When you hear a word whose meaning you are not sure of, write that word down, look it up as soon as possible, and write the definition on the same card. Use that word twice in the same week that you looked it up.

Additional Exercises: Primary and Secondary Meaning of Lexical Items

1. Select any two sentences from "How to Order Fast Food" or "How to Thread a Needle." Refer to the transcripts for the sentences you select. Analyze each sentence and determine which words are used in their primary sense and which are used in a secondary sense.

Additional Exercises at the Word Level: Compounds and Collocations

2. List ten compound words. Do the components of each of these words reveal the meaning of the compound?

____

____

____

____

____

____

____

____

____

3. List ten collocations. What would happen if you reversed the order of the words in the collocation?

____

____

____

____

____

____

____

Additional Exercises: Antonyms

4. Refer back to all of the underlined words in the exercises in this unit. In each utterance, replace the underlined word with an antonym, or word which is opposite in meaning to the underlined word. How does this affect the overall sense of the utterances?

Progress Tracking Sheet

This sheet is designed to help you keep track of which exercises you have completed and how well you have done on these exercises. See page 13 (Teacher's Guide page 20) for a full description of how to use the Progress Tracking Sheet.

This unit's Progress Tracking Sheet covers real-time exercises 3.3 to 3.5.

Exercise Number	Date	First Performance	Study Questions	Follow-up Activity	Questions and Reminders	Date	Second Performance
Exercise 3.3 Quantitative							
Qualitative							
Exercise 3.4 Quantitative							
Qualitative							
Exercise 3.5 Quantitative							
Qualitative							
Quantitative Totals							

UNIT
4

Paraphrasing Propositions

Introduction

Larson (1984, p. 415) writes, "Paraphrase is a restating of the same information in another way, sometimes with the addition of bits of information." Paraphrasing propositions means that you restate an entire idea unit in a different way. Paraphrasing in its strictest sense is an intralingual skill. Intralingual means within one language, and does not involve two languages. People who are developing skills in a specific language often work to find various ways to say the same thing in order to strengthen their language skills. For example, a new speaker of English may use an entire phrase to express a single word if they do not know that word. This new speaker might say, "the machine which puts on paper, the information from your computer screen" instead of the word "printer." Topics in this unit on paraphrasing propositions include illocutionary force, ambiguity, and unpacking propositions.

Illocutionary Force

The illocutionary force of a message allows the listener to know if the message was intended to function as a statement, command, or question. According to Larson (1984), illocutionary force is often conveyed by intonation in English. In other words, the tone of voice used by the speaker will allow the listener to know if the utterance "When are you going to take out the garbage?" is really a question or a statement regarding a chore that has not been done yet, but should have been done. The fact that this utterance is really a rhetorical question is indicated through the intonation pattern used when it is spoken.

Practice in preserving illocutionary force is important because it allows you to determine if the paraphrase has the same impact on the listener as the original message. Preserving the illocutionary force means that even though the message is transferred from one language to another, the impact of the message on the listener(s) in the source language should be roughly equivalent to the impact of the message on listeners in the target language.

Ambiguity

Ambiguity is the linguistic feature that can create uncertainty in the mind of the listener. This happens when the utterance has more than one possible meaning. Usually, the linguistic and social context in which the utterance occurs can disambiguate the word or phrase, but not always. It is very important to disambiguate any utterance in the source language before translating it. If an utterance is intentionally ambiguous in the source language, then the interpreter must also create an utterance in the target language that conveys approximately the same amount of ambiguity. For example, in some legal situations, the interrogator may intend to confuse the person being questioned and so uses ambiguous or unclear language. Ideally, the interpreter conveys the same amount of ambiguity. In reality, sometimes the utterance cannot be interpreted until the interpreter knows which meaning is intended.

Ambiguity can occur at the lexical level or at the phrase level. The words bed, pilot, free, plant, on, about, and many others have more than one meaning. The intended meaning is usually revealed by the context. A phrase which is often used to show ambiguity at the phrase level is "the toy car and truck are in the driveway." This phrase could be paraphrased, as either "there are two toys in the driveway" or "one toy car and one truck are in the driveway." The context alone will not be enough to disambiguate this phrase, but one way to go about finding which meaning is intended is to paraphrase the original into the two or more possible meanings that can be found.

Most interpreters have had the experience of realizing, after the fact, that they misunderstood a portion of the meaning of the speaker's message. The high stress levels that accompany most interpretation assignments often prevent interpreters from quickly realizing that the utterance was ambiguous and that more than one meaning is possible. When the stress of the situation has passed, the assignment is completed, and the interpreter is no longer in the interpreting situation, the interpreter may suddenly realize, with a sinking feeling, that he or she conveyed the wrong message. This error could be due to not noticing the ambiguity and not dealing with it in real-time by asking questions to clarify the meaning. Hopefully, the frequency of the occurrence of this kind of situation is reduced by practicing paraphrasing information in exercise format, removed from real interpretation situations. Later these skills can be applied in real-world situations in interpretation settings.

A certain amount of ability to tolerate ambiguity is required. Not all words or phrases that are ambiguous to the interpreter can be clarified. More mature students and interpreters may be able to tolerate greater amounts of ambiguity. Ambiguity can arise for a number of reasons. The speaker may not really know what point he or she wishes to make. The speaker may even intend to be ambiguous. Sometimes it will be difficult for the interpreter to follow the speaker's line of reasoning and this can create uncertainty in the mind of the interpreter. The speaker may not follow a prepared text. The speaker may not show or tell the interpreter how the ideas being presented are related. In all of these situations the interpreter must convey the information as best they can. It may be necessary for the interpreter to stop the speaker and ask for clarification.

Unpacking Propositions

When Larson (1984) uses the term "unpacking" she means that within each word, it is possible to find more than one concept. The same is true of propositions or idea units. It is important for the interpreter to be able to quickly see as many relevant and possible ideas within each proposition as possible. This is a good beginning point for hypothesis testing. In other words, when an interpreter hears a phrase, they should quickly try to see the various meanings that could be included in that phrase and then discard those hypotheses that are not relevant to the current linguistic and social context. For example, given the phrase "The mother is feeding her baby" as an exercise, the following reasonable propositions can be unpacked or delineated.

There is a woman.

There is a baby.

The woman may be the baby's mother.

The baby may be the child of the woman.

There is baby food.

The woman knows the baby is hungry.

The baby is hungry.

The following list of propositions could *not* be unpacked from the original because they assume too much information. These propositions may be true but their relevance cannot be determined from the original utterance.

The baby is a boy.

The baby is a girl.

The baby is allergic to eggs.

The mother likes feeding the baby.

The baby hates to be fed.

The baby wants the father to feed it.

The mother is late for work.

The practice of unpacking propositions reveals important ideas and can improve paraphrasing skills because this kind of exercise can help you see which ideas are really part of the concept and which are not.

The Role of Paraphrasing in the Interpretation Process

According to deGroot (1997, p. 52),"Paraphrasing involves the conversion of a message expressed in given language into an equivalent message in the same language but worded differently." deGroot goes on to point out that when paraphrasing between two spoken forms of language is done simultaneously, the demands of this task appear to be similar to those of simultaneous interpretation. "Not only do the two tasks share the requirement of simultaneous comprehension and production of speech, but unlike shadowing, they also both require a translation act, an act of recoding the same content in a different form." Other authors (Malakoff and Hakuta, 1991) suggest that intralingual paraphrasing is even more difficult than translation or interpretation because a larger vocabulary is required to perform paraphrasing acts in a single language.

An indicator of a good interpretation is that it maintains the dynamics of the source language. The dynamics are conveyed thorough illocutionary force. This means that the listener will receive the same impact, response, or emotional effect in an interpreted message as the person who heard the message in its original language. This is the ideal. However, in situations such as interpreting for a joke or other information that is heavily culturally laden, it is very difficult to maintain the same level of illocutionary force in the target language.

Sometimes a single lexical item in the source language must be expressed in several words in the target language, such as when there is no single lexical equivalent in the target language. The converse of this can also be true. These situations call on paraphrasing skills to give the message the greatest impact. Paraphrasing is also used when idioms occur in the source language and do not have an equivalent expression in the target language. In that case the meaning of the idiom must be reexpressed in the target language in a way that is meaningful in that language.

Because there is generally not a one-to-one correspondence of lexical items across language boundaries, interpreters must have a variety of techniques they can use to accurately convey the meaning of the message from the source language into the target language. One of the most useful techniques that should be practiced with conscious effort is the ability to quickly paraphrase a message within the source language and then to translate that paraphrased version of the message. During the interpretation process, this paraphrase and subsequent interpretation of the paraphrase must be done with the highest possible speed and accuracy. In the actual process of simultaneous interpretation, it is possible that you might not realize that sometimes you paraphrase the source language before interpreting it.

Paraphrasing Techniques that Can Be Used in the Interpretation Process

Occasionally during the interpretation process, an adequate interpretation does not appear in the mind of the interpreter. One good way to get out of such a "linguistic box" or problem is to paraphrase the original sentence and then interpret the paraphrased version. It is very important that the paraphrased version maintain the meaning of the original. For example, "There is a woman getting ready to go out the door" could be paraphrased as "A lady is prepared to leave via the exit." This paraphrase may sound a bit awkward, but it does not distort the meaning. If I were to paraphrase the original sentence as "A lady has gone out the door" I have changed the meaning by using a past tense verb.

A second paraphrasing technique is to substitute one word at a time in the original sentence by finding synonyms. Again, this may lead to an awkward-sounding paraphrase, but that may not be a problem if the paraphrase maintains the meaning of the original utterance and provides you with a good point for beginning the interpretation. A word of caution: This does *not* mean that you should *translate* each word in a sentence in order to arrive at the interpretation. Since most languages do not have corresponding lexical items, a word-for-word translation can rarely preserve the meaning of the original utterance.

A third method of paraphrasing is to change the message from active to passive voice or vice versa. For example, this sentence is in the passive voice: "The door was closed by the boy." It can be paraphrased by changing it to active voice: "The boy closed the door." When working from English to ASL, this will be a particularly useful strategy. First, paraphrase the passive voice into active voice and then interpret the paraphrased version of the sentence.

A fourth possibility is reversing the clauses within the sentence. This can only be used if it does not change the meaning. For example, "Fred got sick from a tick bite in July and later in the summer he went to the doctor" can be paraphrased as "Fred went to the doctor last summer after he got sick after he was bitten by a tick." The sentence "John got up early, had breakfast, and then went out to do his errands" cannot be paraphrased as "John did his errands, had breakfast, and got up early." The meaning is not preserved in the second paraphrase. When the order of events is important to the meaning, then the order of events must appear in the same order in the paraphrase.

A fifth technique is to paraphrase the utterance into a more general form than the original sentence and still not skew the meaning. You can review the section on specific and general words to reinforce this topic. If the paraphrase is more specific, then the original meaning may be skewed. For example, "A baker is getting his bowls, rolling pin, pans, and measuring cups out" can be paraphrased as "A baker is getting his baking utensils ready to use." The word "utensils" is a more general word and can include the items mentioned in the original sentence. The sentence is "The baker is pouring batter into a pan" cannot be paraphrased as "The man is putting batter into a springform pan." A springform pan is a specific type of pan and it is not implied by the original sentence. An acceptable paraphrase is "A man who knows how to bake is putting batter into a container."

A sixth way to paraphrase is to change the message from figurative language to nonfigurative language. Figurative language includes idioms, which must be paraphrased before they can be translated. For example, the idiom "I am all thumbs" is figurative language and is difficult to interpret. If you interpret this literally or in a word-for-word fashion, the meaning will be lost. First you must paraphrase the idiom to "I am clumsy" or "I am not good with my hands" and then interpret it. The phrase "I am boiling" is another example of figurative language. You must interpret the meaning, not the form. The meaning is "I am very hot" or "I am very angry" depending on the context.

These six basic ways to approach paraphrasing: changing verb tense, word-for-word substitution, changing from or to active or passive voice, changing the order of the propositions, moving from specific to more general terms, and moving from figurative to nonfigurative language are all ways that you can improve your linguistic flexibility. Increased linguistic flexibility helps form a strong foundation for accurate simultaneous interpretation skills as well as excellent self-expression skills.

Discussion Questions

Discuss the following questions with your students to promote insight and increase awareness of the importance of paraphrasing proposition skills as they relate to the interpretation process.

1. *How does an understanding of paraphrasing propositions in English relate to the interpretation process?*

   Practice in paraphrasing propositions can increase the range of grammatical constructions that are quickly available for the interpreter to use. When paraphrasing, it is important to preserve the meaning of the original message. Since the simultaneous interpretation process is so cognitively demanding, it is important to reduce cognitive effort wherever possible. One way to help reduce the effort needed is to practice specific components within the interpretation process. Be sure to point out to your students that it is necessary to practice paraphrasing within each of the languages that will be used in the interpretation process. Some students may feel that if English is their first language, they do not need to practice paraphrasing. However, practice in this skill can provide great linguistic flexibility for the interpreter. It is quite common for students to find themselves repeating instead of paraphrasing. It will be important for you as the teacher to help students see clearly the difference between repetition and paraphrasing.

2.   *How would you describe your ability to paraphrase propositions?*

Ask this question before and after the practice exercises and see if students feel that their skills improve and if they have greater confidence in them. One difference that should surface is the difference between repetition and paraphrasing. Most students improve with increased focus and practice. Confidence in the ability to restate ideas quickly is a benefit to the interpreter. Rapid and reliable propositional paraphrasing skills are not automatic, but rather must be learned and practiced. Asking this question before and after the exercises highlights the difference between having the impression of having the skill and actually having the skill.

3.   *What will happen if the interpreter does not have rapid, reliable propositional paraphrasing skills?*

When the interpreter does not have quick access to various ways to express the same concept, then interpreter is limited in linguistic flexibility. When linguistic flexibility is limited, the richness of the product of the interpretation is compromised. For example, if an interpreter is working from ASL to English and knows only one way to interpret a phrase the interpreter's work into English is limited in scope.

4.   *What are some acceptable methods for paraphrasing?*

Here are a few methods that can be used in paraphrasing.

a.   *Replace lexical items with synonyms.*

b.   *Change from active to passive voice.*

c.   *Change the order of phrases.*

d.   *Use more general or more specific terms.*

e.   *Unpack figurative language and restate in nonfigurative language.*

Paraphrasing Propositions Exercises

EXERCISE 4.1

Feeding the Baby

Explain to the students that answering questions written in the workbook does not have the same time pressure as real-time responses. Give an example of repeating as compared to paraphrasing so that the students do not use repetition instead of paraphrasing. The overall length of the paraphrase should be roughly equivalent to the original. If it is much shorter than the original it may be a summary instead of a paraphrase. If the paraphrase is much longer than the original, it may be more like an expansion on a topic than a paraphrase. Some answers are provided as a guide for you. Other answers may be acceptable. The paraphrase may be less idiomatic than the original.

Directions

Student Workbook page 135

The video selection is approximately two minutes long. You will do this exercise in the workbook first and then in real-time. Do the study questions and follow-up. You will need three colored pencils, red, blue, and black.

Workbook Propositional Paraphrasing

In this section you work from the printed version of the transcripts, not from the videotape. Read the title of this selection and paraphrase it in writing below the printed title. Then, read each of Diana's responses and provide a paraphrase of each of her responses. Write your paraphrase below each of the sentences in the transcript. Read each of Leslie's responses and paraphrase each of her responses by writing your paraphrase below her response on the transcript.

Transcript for *Feeding the Baby*

Write your paraphrase of the title here.

Baby's feeding time

Diana's responses to Feeding the Baby:

Diana 1   A woman is getting ready to feed her baby.

There is a baby about to be fed by a woman. (Change in order of propositions)

Diana 2   She begins to feed her baby.

She starts feeding her child. (Paraphrase by lexical substitution)

Diana 3   By the time the feeding is over, the baby's face is covered
with food.

The baby's face is covered with food by the end of the feeding. (Change in order

of propositions)

Leslie's responses to Feeding the Baby:

Leslie 1   There is a woman in quite fancy clothes getting ready to feed
her son or daughter some dark, pureed food.

A boy or girl is about to be fed some pureed, dark food by a dressed up woman.

(Change in order of propositions, active to passive)

Leslie 2   Next we see the child resisting a bit as the mother puts the food
in the child's mouth.

When the mother puts food in the baby's mouth, the baby resists a little. (Change

in order of propositions)

Leslie 3   Now we see the child covered with pureed food and the mother smiling proudly.

The mother smiles proudly and the baby is covered with pureed food. (Change in order of propositions)

Real-Time Propositional Paraphrasing

After you complete the paraphrase for each speaker's responses, do a real-time paraphrase for each utterance. Locate this selection on your video and turn on your recording device to record your responses as you paraphrase each of Diana's responses immediately after you hear them. Do this by listening to one sentence and then stopping the videotape when you hear the beep. Then say your paraphrased version of the sentence. Follow this procedure to do the real-time paraphrasing of Leslie's utterances. Be sure to record your work so you can transcribe it. After you have recorded your answers, transcribe your answers so you can compare them easily to Diana and Leslie's transcripts.

The student paraphrases for real-time may be the same or different from those in the workbook version, but should not be direct repetitions of the original text.

Transcribe your real-time paraphrases here.

Diana   1. ____

____

2. ____

____

3. ____

____

Leslie   1. ____

____

2. ____

____

3. ____

   ____

Study Questions

Use red to compare your responses to Diana's. Use blue to compare your responses to Leslie's. Use black to underline differences in illocutionary force.

1. Compare Diana's responses with your workbook and real-time paraphrasing of her utterances. Do all three, the original and your two paraphrases, convey the same meaning? If not, circle in red the parts of your paraphrase that changed the meaning.

    Questions 1 and 2 relate to meaning and are good ones for group discussion. It is important to allow students many opportunities to see how many different meanings could possibly be contained in a phrase. These differences become more apparent in discussions. It is likely that students will be better able to see where the meaning is or is not preserved by engaging in discussions with each other and with you. Provide time for students to express their reasoning for why the meaning is or is not changed by the paraphrase.

2. Compare Leslie's responses with your workbook and real-time paraphrasing of her utterances. Do all three, the original and your two paraphrases, convey the same meaning? If not circle in blue the parts of your paraphrase that changed the meaning.

3. Check each of your paraphrases of Diana's utterances and see if the illocutionary force of each remains the same. If not, underline in black the parts of the paraphrase that cause a change in the illocutionary force.

    The paraphrase should have the same impact on the listener as the original.

4. Check each of your paraphrases of Leslie's utterances and see if the illocutionary force of each remains the same. If not, underline with two black lines the parts of the paraphrase that caused a change in the illocutionary force.

5. Check all of your responses, workbook and real-time, for ambiguity. If you find any instances of ambiguity, paraphrase again so that ambiguity is reduced. Write your new response.

____

____

____

____

In some cases the original may be ambiguous. In such cases the paraphrase cannot be less ambiguous than the original. The paraphrase should not be more ambiguous than the original.

Five-Step Follow-up

Step 1   Observation:

Review your answers and make sure you complete all parts of the exercise.

Step 2   Selection

Select the portions that you circled in either red or blue. These are the parts of your paraphrases that do not have the same meaning as the original sentence. Choose a total of three examples to analyze.

Select the portions that you underlined. These are the parts of your paraphrase that do not have the same illocutionary force as the original sentence. Choose a total of three examples to analyze.

Step 3   Analysis

Using the three selections that you have circled in step 2, determine which part of the form of the paraphrase changed the meaning. Redo the paraphrase so that the original meaning is preserved. For example, Leslie's sentence Leslie 1 is "There is a woman in quite fancy clothes getting ready to feed her son or daughter some dark, pureed food." My paraphrase is "A very dressed up lady is opening a jar of baby food for her baby." My paraphrase changes the meaning because "getting ready to feed" does not necessarily mean opening a jar of baby food. The original sentence does not say that the son or daughter is a baby. A more accurate paraphrase is "A well-dressed lady is preparing to feed her boy or girl some food that is not solid and is dark in color."

____

____

____

____

____

____

Using the portions of the transcript that you have underlined in step 2, look for which section of your paraphrases have different illocutionary force than the original. For example, Leslie's response Leslie 2 is "Next we see the child resisting a bit as the mother puts the food in the child's mouth." My paraphrase is "Now the child is shown refusing to eat the food." The illocutionary impacts of "resisting" and "refusing" are quite different. "Refusing" is much stronger than "resisting." Describe how these differences in illocutionary force affect meaning.

____

____

____

____

Step 4   Assessment

Review your work in steps 2 and 3 and determine if you are able to accurately paraphrase propositions. If you are not sure, then go to the original sentences and replace the words one at a time with synonyms. Try using passive voice to help you create paraphrases that do not change the meaning. Write a description of how your awareness of the importance of accuracy in paraphrasing has changed as a result of doing this exercise.

____

____

____

____

Step 5   Action

You can take further action to improve your paraphrasing skills by selecting the remaining parts of the transcript for deeper analysis and revision, following the steps in the study questions and follow-up.

EXERCISE 4.2

Peeling Potatoes

Directions

**Student Workbook
page 140**

This selection is less than two minutes long. You will do this exercise in the workbook first and then in real-time. Then do the study questions and follow-up. The four parts of this exercise are workbook paraphrasing, recording your real-time responses, answering the study questions, and completing the follow-up. You will need three colored pencils, red, blue, and black.

Workbook Propositional Paraphrasing

In this section you will work from the printed version of the transcripts, not from the videotape. Read the title of this selection and paraphrase it in writing below the printed title. Then, read each of Diana's responses and provide a paraphrase of each of her responses. Write your paraphrase below each of the sentences in the transcript. Read each of Leslie's responses and paraphrase each of her responses by writing your paraphrase below her response on the transcript.

Transcript for *Peeling Potatoes*

Paraphrase the title here.

Removing potato skins

Diana's responses to Peeling Potatoes:

Diana 1   A woman has two pans in front of her.

There are two pans in front of a woman. (Change order of phrases)

Diana 2   She begins to peel some potatoes.

She starts removing the potato skins. (Paraphrase via lexical substitution)

Diana 3 She puts the peelings in one pan and the potatoes in the other.

She puts the potatoes in one pan and the skins in the other. (Change order of

 propositions and lexical substitution)

Leslie's responses to Peeling Potatoes:

Leslie 1 There is a woman getting ready to peel potatoes.

A woman is about to peel potatoes. (Lexical substitution)

Leslie 2 She is peeling the skins into a large pot.

She peels the skins into a large pot. (Lexical substitution)

Leslie 3 Next we see her putting the whole peeled potatoes into
     another pot.

Then, in another pot, she puts the whole, peeled potatoes. (Change order

 of phrases)

Real-Time Propositional Paraphrasing

After you complete the paraphrase for each speaker's responses, do a real-time paraphrase for each utterance. Locate this selection on your video and turn on your recording device to record your responses as you paraphrase each of Diana's responses immediately after you hear it. Do this by listening to one sentence, stopping the videotape when you hear the beep, and then saying your paraphrased version of the sentence. Follow this procedure to do the real-time paraphrasing of Leslie's utterances. Be sure to record your work so you can transcribe it. After you have recorded your answers, transcribe your answers so you can compare them easily to Diana and Leslie's transcripts.

Note that Diana's and Leslie's responses are not compared directly to each other in this exercise. Each speaker uses a different form of expression in spoken English to describe what she saw and they were not attempting to paraphrase each other's work.

Diana   1. ____

____

2. ____

____

3. ____

____

Leslie   1. ____

____

2. ____

____

3. ____

____

Study Questions

Use red to compare your responses to Diana's responses. Use blue to compare your responses to Leslie's responses. Use black to underline differences in illocutionary force.

1. Compare Diana's responses with your workbook and real-time paraphrasing of her utterances. Do all three, the original and your two paraphrases, convey the same meaning? If not, circle in red the parts of your paraphrase that changed the meaning.

See previous exercise for comments for the teacher.

2. Compare Leslie's responses with your workbook and real-time paraphrasing of her utterances. Do all three, the original and your two paraphrases, convey the same meaning? If not, circle in blue the parts of your paraphrase that changed the meaning.

3. Check each of your paraphrases of Diana's utterances and see if the illocutionary force of each remains the same. If not, underline in black the parts of the paraphrase that caused a change in the illocutionary force.

4. Check each of your paraphrases of Leslie's utterances and see if the illocutionary force of each remains the same. If not, underline with two black lines the parts of the paraphrase that caused a change in the illocutionary force.

5. Check all of your responses, workbook and real-time, for ambiguity. If you find any instances of ambiguity, paraphrase again so that ambiguity is reduced. Write your new response.

Five-Step Follow-up

Step 1   Observation

Review your answers and make sure you complete all parts of the exercise.

Step 2   Selection

Select the portions that you circle in either red or blue. These are the parts of your paraphrases that do not have the same meaning as the original sentence. Choose a total of three examples to analyze.

Select the portions that you underlined. These are the parts of your paraphrase that do not have the same illocutionary force as the original sentence. Choose a total of three examples to analyze.

Step 3   Analysis

Using the three selections that you circled in step 2, determine which part of the form of the paraphrase changed the meaning. Redo the paraphrase so that the original meaning is preserved.

____

____

____

____

Using the portions of the transcript that you underlined in step 2, determine which section of your paraphrases have different illocutionary force than the original. Describe how these differences in illocutionary force affect meaning.

Step 4   Assessment

Review your work in steps 2 and 3 and determine if you can accurately paraphrase propositions. If you are not sure, then go to the original sentences and replace the words one at a time with synonyms. Try using passive voice or active voice to help you create paraphrases that do not change the meaning. Write a description of how your awareness of the importance of accuracy in paraphrasing has changed as a result of doing this exercise.

Step 5   Action

You can take further action to improve your paraphrasing skills by selecting the remaining parts of the transcript for deeper analysis and revision, following the steps in the study questions and follow-up.

EXERCISE 4.3

Breaking Eggs

Directions

Student Workbook
page 145

This selection is less than two minutes long. You will do this exercise in the workbook first and then in real-time. Answer the study questions and complete the follow-up. The four parts of this exercise are recording your responses in the workbook, real-time responses, answering the study questions, and doing the follow-up. You will need three colored pencils, red, blue, and black.

Workbook Paraphrasing

In this section you work from the printed version of the transcripts, not from the videotape. Read the title of this selection and paraphrase it in writing below the printed title. Then, read each of Diana's responses and provide a paraphrase of each of her responses. Write your paraphrase below each of the sentences in the transcript. Read each of Leslie's responses and paraphrase each of her responses by writing your paraphrase below her response on the transcript.

Transcript *Breaking Eggs*

Write your paraphrase of the title here.

Cracking Eggs Open

Diana's responses to Breaking Eggs:

Diana 1   A woman is cracking an egg over a bowl.

There is a bowl and a woman is cracking an egg into it.

Diana 2   The egg is dripping into the bowl.

The egg drips in the bowl.

Diana 3   Now the egg is in the bowl and the woman is holding the shells.

Now, the woman is holding the shells and the bowl contains the eggs.

Leslie's responses to Breaking Eggs:

Leslie 1   There is a woman breaking eggs into a glass bowl. She picks up
the first egg.

There is a glass bowl into which a woman is breaking eggs. The first egg is picked

up by the woman. (Keep the separate sentences in the same order in which

they occurred. Note that this paraphrase tends to put more emphasis on the

egg rather than the woman. Another option would be to say "The woman

picks up the egg.")

Leslie 2   She cracks the first egg.

The first egg is cracked by the woman. (This passive construction is awkward, but

is still a paraphrase. The paraphrase emphasizes that the egg is the recipient

of the action.)

Leslie 3   She is holding two of the pieces of the broken egg in her hand.

In her hands, she is holding two of the pieces of the broken egg.

Real-Time Propositional Paraphrasing

After you complete the workbook paraphrase for each speaker's responses, do real-time paraphrase for each utterance. Locate this selection on your video and turn on your recording device to record your responses as you paraphrase each of Diana's responses immediately after you hear it. Do this by listening to one sentence, then stop the video tape after you hear the beep, and then say your paraphrased version of the sentence. Follow this procedure to do the real-time paraphrasing of Leslie's utterances. Be sure to record your work so you can transcribe it. After you have recorded your answers, transcribe your answers so you can compare them easily to Diana and Leslie's transcripts.

Note that Diana's and Leslie's responses are not compared directly to each other in this exercise. Each speaker used a different form of expression in spoken English to describe what she saw and they were not attempting to paraphrase each other's work.

Transcribe your real-time paraphrases here.

Diana

1. _______________________________________

____

2. _______________________________________

____

3. _______________________________________

____

Leslie

1. _______________________________________

____

2. _______________________________________

____

3. _______________________________________

____

Study Questions

Use red to compare your responses to Diana's responses. Use blue to compare your responses to Leslie's responses. Use black to underline differences in illocutionary force.

1. Compare Diana's responses with your workbook and real-time paraphrasing of her utterances. Do all three, the original and your two paraphrases, convey the same meaning? If not, circle in red the parts of your paraphrase that changed the meaning.

2. Compare Leslie's responses with your workbook and real-time paraphrasing of her utterances. Do all three, the original and your two paraphrases, convey the same meaning? If not, circle in blue the parts of your paraphrase that changed the meaning.

3. Check each of your paraphrases of Diana's utterances and see if the illocutionary force of each remains the same. If not, underline in black the parts of the paraphrase that caused a change in the illocutionary force.

4. Check each of your paraphrases of Leslie's utterances and see if the illocutionary force of each remains the same. If not, underline with two black lines the parts of the paraphrase that caused a change in the illocutionary force.

5. Check all of your responses, workbook and real-time, for ambiguity. If you find any instances of ambiguity, paraphrase again so that ambiguity is reduced. Write your new response.

____

____

____

____

____

____

____

____

Five-Step Follow-up

Step 1   **Observation**

Review your answers and make sure you complete all parts of the exercise.

Step 2   **Selection**

Select the portions that you circled in either red or blue. These are the parts of your paraphrases that do not have the same meaning as the original sentence. Choose a total of three examples to analyze.

Select the portions that you underlined. These are the parts of your paraphrase that do not have the same illocutionary force as the original sentence. Choose a total of three examples to analyze.

Step 3   **Analysis**

Using the three selections that you have circled in step 2, determine which part of the form of the paraphrase changed the meaning. Redo the paraphrase so that the original meaning is preserved. For example, Diana's sentence Diana 1 is "A woman is cracking an egg over a bowl." My paraphrase is "A lady is cracking an egg into a container." This is an acceptable paraphrase because "container" is a more general word than "bowl."

Leslie's sentence Leslie 1 is "There is a woman breaking eggs into a glass bowl. She picks up the first egg." My paraphrase is "A lady is cracking eggs into a mixing bowl. She has the first egg in her hand." This is an acceptable paraphrase because a "mixing bowl" is a more general word than "glass bowl" and picking up an egg implies that it is done with the hand.

____

____

____

____

____

____

____

____

Using the portions of the transcript that you underlined in step 2, determine which section of your paraphrases have different illocutionary force than the original. For example, Diana's first response Diana 1 is "A woman is cracking an egg over a bowl." My paraphrase is "A lady is smashing eggs into a container." The words "cracking" and "smashing" are not equivalent in illocutionary force. "Smashing" is a much stronger word than "cracking." Describe how these differences in illocutionary force affect meaning.

Step 4   Assessment

Review your work in steps two and three and determine if you can accurately paraphrase propositions. If you are not sure, then go to the original sentences and replace the words one at a time with synonyms. Try using passive voice or active voice to help you create paraphrases that do not change the meaning. Write a description of how your awareness of the importance of accuracy in paraphrasing has changed as a result of doing this exercise.

Step 5   Action

You can take further action to improve your paraphrasing skills by selecting the remaining parts of the transcript for deeper analysis and revision, following the steps in the study questions and follow-up.

Additional Exercises: Unpacking Propositions

1. Read Diana's and Leslie's responses to "Feeding the Baby." Unpack each of
    the propositions. List as many propositions as you can. The propositions
    must be both relevant and possible. Write them in the space provided.

Diana   ____

             ____

             ____

             ____

             ____

             ____

             ____

Leslie   ____

             ____

             ____

             ____

             ____

             ____

             ____

             ____

             ____

2. Read Diana's and Leslie's responses to "Peeling Potatoes." Unpack each of
    the propositions. List as many propositions as you can. The propositions
    must be both relevant and possible. Write them in the space provided.

Diana   ____

____

____

____

____

____

____

Leslie   ____

____

____

____

____

____

____

____

3. Read Diana's and Leslie's responses to "Breaking Eggs." Unpack each of the propositions. List as many propositions as you can. The propositions must be both relevant and possible. Write them in the space provided.

Diana

____

____

____

____

____

____

____

____

Leslie

____

____

____

____

____

____

____

____

Progress Tracking Sheet

This sheet is designed to help you keep track of which exercises you have completed and how well you have done on these exercises. See page 13 (Teacher's Guide page 20) for a full description of how to use the Progress Tracking Sheet.

Exercise Number	Date	First Performance	Study Questions	Follow-up Activity	Questions and Reminders	Date	Second Performance
Exercise 4.1 Quantitative							
Qualitative							
Exercise 4.2 Quantitative							
Qualitative							
Exercise 4.3 Quantitative							
Qualitative							
Quantitative Totals							

UNIT 5

Paraphrasing Discourse

Introduction

Paraphrasing at the discourse level is restating a story or text in words different than those in the original. Review the information in Unit 4 on paraphrasing propositions. All of the constraints of paraphrasing information at the sentence level apply to paraphrasing at the discourse level. A paraphrase of discourse-level text should contain the same information as the original, but is not an exact repetition. In some cases the order of information must be preserved exactly, as in giving directions or instructions. In other kinds of texts, the exact order of information can be less crucial. In cases where the order of information is less crucial, the paraphrase need not necessarily preserve the order of information.

In general, when practicing paraphrasing, it is advisable to keep the information in the paraphrase in the same order as the information in the original. If the interpreter believes that the order of events is inconsequential, that may change the cause and effect relationship between events in the text. It is preferable to reduce the amount of decision making that the interpreter must do. Training oneself to keep the events in the same order and relationship to each other is one way to reduce errors in interpretation.

A paraphrased text should contain as many of the features found in the original as possible. For example, if the original had an introduction and conclusion section, then so should the paraphrase. The approximate length of the text should be roughly the same in the paraphrase as in the original. The illocutionary force should not be altered in the paraphrase. Main and supporting details should be preserved as well.

Two things determine the actual form of the paraphrase. The first is the comprehension of the source text by the person doing the paraphrase. The second major factor is that person's ability in expressive language. The greater the range of expressive language, the better the paraphrase. Aptitudes in comprehension and expression contribute to the facility with which the paraphrase is accomplished.

This unit includes information on the following topics: question forms and functions, and idiomatic expressions.

Question Forms and Functions

Quick and accurate identification of the various forms and functions of language is essential to rapid and accurate paraphrasing. Statements generally convey information. Commands order someone to do something. A more complicated situation arises in relation to question forms. Kearsely (1976) provides a good summary on questions and their forms and functions. He says that the intonation and gestures that accompany a question as well as the syntax can help identify question forms and functions. Some questions seek to gain information, such as "What would you like for lunch?" Other questions serve to provide information. In the question, "Are you ready to order?" the information that the waiter is ready to take your order is conveyed. Rhetorical questions generally function as statements of information or clarification rather than attempts to gain information. Sometimes questions serve to draw attention to a point. For example, in a lecture setting, the teacher may ask, "Is everyone ready to take the quiz?" Occasionally, questions are repeated by the listener back to the questioner. When this happens, the purpose is usually to buy some time rather than ask the information of the questioner. This is called "echoic" questioning.

Question *forms* include the following types of questions:

1. Yes/No Questions. These require a "yes" or "no" response.

2. Wh Questions. These seek information and begin with a "wh" word such as what, who, why, where or when.

3. Rhetorical Questions. These sound like questions, but function as attention getting strategies or to convey information.

Question *functions* include the following:

1. Some questions seek information that can be answered with yes or no. This type of question is called a closed question. For example, "Can I borrow your bus schedule?" This question can be answered with only a limited number of responses. The usual answers will be "yes", "no" or "maybe." Another possible answer is "I'm using it now." This answer functions as a "no."

2. Some questions require more of an answer than just yes or no. These are called open-ended questions. An example of an open-ended question is "How do you feel about buying a used car?" The answer can include a wide variety of information, but not a yes or no answer.

3. Rhetorical questions bring attention to a point. They do not really seek information even though they sound like questions. An example of a rhetorical question is a teacher saying to the class "Is everyone ready to take the test?" The function is to bring attention to the fact that it is time to take the test.

Idiomatic Expressions

Idiomatic expressions occur in most languages. According to Beekman and Callow (1974, p. 121), "Idioms are expressions of at least two words which cannot be understood literally and which function as a unit semantically." English has many idioms that are used in everyday speech. One example is "Don't let the cat out of the bag." This means do not tell the secret or give information to others. Here are some examples of idioms—rush into print, step into a practice, fly into a passion, spring into action, jump into a fight, dive into a book, wade into adversity, quiet as a mouse, keep an eye on someone, and he is hopping mad.

Idioms cannot be understood by analyzing each word in the idiom separately, nor can they be translated or interpreted literally. Instead, they must first be paraphrased, or restated in the source language and then translated or interpreted. A paraphrased idiom may sound awkward or may sound like an explanation. Nevertheless, this kind of paraphrase provides a good starting point for an interpretation of an idiom.

Sometimes the target language has an expression that roughly captures the meaning of the idiomatic expression in the source language, and in such instances, those equivalent phrases can be used.

The Role of Paraphrasing at the Discourse Level in the Interpretation Process

Rendering the same message in a different form is often called restructuring, whether it is in the same language or not. Practice in paraphrasing or retelling provides direct experience in restructuring information. Strictly speaking, the term "restructuring" is most often used to refer to the utterances created in the target language after the message has been translated. In the interpretation process, the message is presented in the source language, perceived, comprehended and translated, and then rendered into a different linguistic form, the target language. One way to develop skills in accurate reconstruction of information is to practice conveying the same information via paraphrasing, or retelling, in your first language. It is best to practice paraphrasing in your first language first and then in your second language.

These two skills, paraphrasing and restructuring, are intimately related, even though the first is an intralingual skill and the second is an interlingual skill. They both require some of the same cognitive skills. Since the process of simultaneous interpretation is far more cognitively demanding than paraphrasing, spending time developing accurate paraphrasing skills can reduce the cognitive load during the interpretation process as skill in the interpretation process is developed.

In this unit, you will practice both workbook and real-time paraphrasing. Workbook paraphrasing means that you have time to listen to the source text and then provide the paraphrase, without immediate time constraints. Practice in workbook paraphrasing allows time for you to reinspect the paraphrase and see that it is accurate in terms of information and order of presentation, before adding the pressure of simultaneity. Real-time paraphrasing, that is, retelling the information immediately after hearing it, is cognitively more demanding than workbook paraphrasing because the amount of time allowed for your response is lessened and because you are responding to a spoken form rather than a written form of the message. This process of moving from workbook to real-time helps develop skills in paraphrasing that lead to greater effectiveness in the simultaneous interpretation process.

It is important to realize that while idioms must be "unpacked" and clearly understood before they are interpreted the most desirable interpretation is an idiomatic interpretation. This means that when rendered into the target language, the message is expressed in its most natural-sounding form. The most natural-sounding form may include using idioms to express an idea. A literal interpretation is less desirable then an idiomatic translation. The literal interpretation is the one that uses a word-for-word approach and often obscures the meaning. An unduly free translation is one that does not preserve the meaning of the original text. For more information on idioms and idiomatic interpretation please consult Larson (1984).

Discussion Questions

Discuss the following questions with your students to promote insight and increase awareness of the importance of the ability to paraphrasing discourse, particularly as this skill relates to the interpretation process.

1. *How does an understanding of paraphrasing discourse in English relate to the interpretation process?*

   The ability to quickly rearrange propositions without changing the meaning is important in interpretation because this skill allows for greater flexibility in finding a good starting point for the translation process. For example, it may be necessary to find a less idiomatic way to express the content and intent of a story or passage. The less idiomatic version is often easier to interpret. Ideally, the interpreter will convey the message into as idiomatic a rendition as possible in the target language.

Be sure to point out that it is necessary to practice this skill within each of the languages that will be used in the interpretation process. Some students may feel that if English is their first language, they do not need to study English during their interpretation studies. Practicing the skill of paraphrasing discourse can provide great linguistic flexibility for the interpreter regardless of language pairs.

2. *Do you feel you have strong discourse paraphrasing skills?*

    Ask this question before and after the drills and see if students feel their skills have improved and if they have greater confidence in them. Most students improve with increased focus and practice. Confidence in ability to find the necessary words quickly will be a benefit to the interpreter. Rapid and reliable paraphrasing skills are not automatic, but rather must be learned and practiced.

3. *What happens if the interpreter does not have rapid, reliable discourse paraphrasing skills? The interpreter who does not have rapid and reliable discourse paraphrasing skills will find it more difficult to find the gist of the speech. Finding the gist of the speech allows the interpreter to organize the ideas as they are presented. Second, the ability to paraphrase may lead to a more reliable interpretation of the message.*

4. *What are some acceptable methods for paraphrasing discourse?*

    Here are a few methods that can be used in paraphrasing discourse. Some of these methods are the same as those used for paraphrasing at the proposition level.

    a. *Replace lexical items with synonyms.*

    b. *Change the order of phrases. This can only be used in discourse-level paraphrase if the change in the order does not change the overall meaning of the passage or paragraph.*

    c. *Change from active to passive voice.*

    d. *Unpack figurative language and restate in nonfigurative language.*

    e. *The overall length of the paraphrased version should approximate that of the original text. Remember that a paraphrase is not a repetition, nor a summary.*

Paraphrasing Discourse Exercises

Decide if you want to conduct these exercises in class, or if you want the students to do them on their own time. The workbook versions of the exercises may be done in a group setting. In order for students do the real-time version of these exercises on their own, they must have their own source tape and workbook. The real-time versions of these exercises can be done in a group setting if each student has a way to record his or her answers without interference from other students.

Read the directions and explain them to the students. Allow time for questions after you give the directions. You should plan on at least five minutes to prepare the students for each exercise. Five minutes should be enough, if you have the group's attention, and if all equipment is ready and in working order. All tapes needed for these exercises must be cued to the correct spot. This includes the source tape and any tapes that will be used for recording.

EXERCISE 5.1

My Visit to Madame Tussauds Wax Museum
ELLA PERKIN

Directions

Student Workbook
page 159

You will do this exercise first in workbook mode and then real-time. Then you will do the study questions and follow-up. You will need a tape recorder and blank tape for your recorder and a red, blue, and black pen or pencil for this exercise.

Workbook Paraphrasing

Begin with workbook paraphrasing. A written transcript in this exercise shows the speaker's words. Refer to the transcript. Read it from start to finish one time and then turn on your recording device and paraphrase the information in the transcript one sentence at a time. Pause between sentences. Keep the features of a good paraphrase in mind. Avoid repeating the selection word for word. A word-for-word repetition is not the same as a paraphrase. Then transcribe your paraphrases in the space provided.

Transcript for *My Visit to Madame Tussauds Wax Museum,* by Ella Perkin

Use this copy of the transcript for your workbook paraphrasing. Write your paraphrase in the blanks provided.

1.   Hi. My name is Ella Perkin and I'm gonna tell you about the time I went to Madame Tussauds Wax Museum in London, England. I went with my brother Tom.

Workbook   *Hello, my name is Ella Perkin. I went to Madame Tussauds wax museum in London, England with my brother Tom and I'd like to tell you about it.*

Real-time   ____

____

2.   It was about 18 months ago—we went to visit my relatives who live in Sheffield, England.

Workbook   *We went to visit my relatives in Sheffield, England, about 18 months ago and that's when we went to the wax museum.*

Real-time   ____

____

3.   However, after about two weeks in Sheffield we got bored and decided to go to London for a few days before we had to go home.

Workbook   *But, we got bored after about two weeks in Sheffield and decided to spend a few days in London before we had to go home.*

Real-time   ____

____

4. We traveled around to many different museums and we saw the Buckingham Palace and the other famous attractions and then we decided to go to Madame Tussauds Max—Wax Museum, which is a museum that has wax models of famous people.

Workbook   *We decided to go to Madame Tussauds wax museum, which has wax models of famous people, after we went to many other museums, Buckingham Palace, and other well-known sites.*

Real-time   ____

5. Some of the people that they had models of were Harrison Ford, the Beatles, they had ones of practically everyone who ever lived in the Royal Family, and many of the past U.S. American presidents.

Workbook   *The museum had models of many past presidents of the U.S., most of the Royal Family, the Beatles, Harrison Ford, among others.*

Real-time   ____

6. And the fun part about it was that you could get your picture taken with all the different wax models, so we got our picture taken with the Beatles, and my brother wanted to get his picture taken with Mr. T from The A Team.

Workbook   *Tom wanted to get his photo taken with Mr. T from the A Team and we both got our picture taken with the Beatles. Getting your picture taken with all the different wax models was one of the fun things you could do there.*

Real-time

____

____

____

7. And so he posed with Mr. T flexing his muscles and we also posed with Harrison Ford. Harrison Ford was in uh, Indiana Jones-type setting, with all these rocks.

Workbook *We posed in an Indiana Jones-type setting that had rocks with Harrison Ford, and Tom posed with Mr. T flexing his muscles. (The text does not reveal which person was flexing their muscles and so the paraphrase should not either.)*

Real-time

____

____

____

8. It was really exciting to be able to go—obviously they didn't look totally real but they were life-size and they also had a section where they showed you how they made the wax models and it was very fun.

Workbook *The museum also had a section where they showed how they made the wax models, which was fun. The life-size wax figures did not look completely realistic, but it was thrilling to go to that part of the museum.*

Real-time

____

____

____

9. I also got my picture taken with Boris Becker, who's one of my favorite tennis players.

Workbook   *I got my picture taken with Boris Becker too, he's one my favorite tennis players.*

Real-time

10. So I had a really good time, and I think it's one of the places that a lot of people probably don't go to when they go to London, 'cause they all want to see Buckingham Palace and the Royal Family, but it was very fun and I would recommend for—to anybody to go there.

Workbook   *Madame Tussauds is one of those places that many people don't go to when they visit London, I think, because they all want to see the Royal Family and Buckingham Palace, but it was really fun and I'd recommend that anyone go there.*

Real-time

Real-Time Paraphrasing

Real-time paraphrasing is the second part of this exercise. Find this selection on your tape. Turn on your recording device and listen until you hear the first beep tone on the videotape. Stop the videotape and record your paraphrase of the phrases you just heard. Repeat this process until you reach the end of the video selection. Remember to use all the features of a good paraphrase mentioned in Unit 4 and this unit. Stop the videotape and your recording device at the end of this selection.

Study Questions

1. Read your workbook paraphrase and compare the transcript of the original sentences to your workbook paraphrase. Is your work a paraphrase or a repetition? Does your paraphrase convey the same meaning as the original?

2. Transcribe your real-time paraphrase. If your paraphrase does not convey the same meaning as the original, use red to circle those parts of your transcript that are skewed in your real-time paraphrase. Is the information in the same order? Use blue to circle information that is correct but is presented in a different order in your paraphrase than in the original. Use black to underline where you added information that was not in the original message.

3. Reexamine both versions of your paraphrase, workbook and real-time, and make a list of the order of events as you conveyed them in each paraphrase. Use the blue circles in your answer to question 2 to help you with this. Compare these lists with each other. Are they the same? Compare these with the original to see if the order of information is the same. Sometimes the order of events can be altered slightly without changing the meaning. Would it change the message if you changed the order of events in this selection?

Workbook	**Real-time**

____

____

____

____

____

____

____

____

____

____

4. Check for question forms in the source and in your workbook and real-time paraphrases. Are there any instances where your paraphrase would have been enhanced by using a question form? If so, put a red question mark on your transcript at that location. Are there places where you use a question form that alters the meaning? If so, put a blue question mark on your transcript at that location.

5. Check the spoken, original text, and both versions of your paraphrase for idiomatic expressions. List any idiomatic expressions that you found in the original text. Did you paraphrase the idioms or repeat the idiomatic expressions? If you repeated any idiomatic expressions instead of paraphrasing them, write out the meaning of the idioms here.

____

____

____

____

Five-Step Follow-up

Step 1   **Observation**

Review your answers and make sure you have completed all parts of the exercise.

Step 2   **Selection**

Select the portions that you circled in red in study question 2. These are the parts of your paraphrases that do not have the same meaning as the original sentence. Choose a total of three examples from your real-time paraphrase to analyze.

Select the portions that you circled in blue in study question 2. These are the parts of your paraphrase that do not have the same order of information as the original sentence. Choose a total of three examples from your real-time paraphrase to analyze.

Step 3   **Analysis**

Using the three selections that you circled in step 2, determine which part of the form of your paraphrase changed the meaning. Redo the paraphrase so that the original meaning is preserved. For example, Ella's sentence is "However, after about two weeks we got bored and decided to go to London for few days before we had to go home." My paraphrase is "We were bored and decided to go to London." This paraphrase does not convey the same meaning as the original because I have left out information. A more accurate paraphrase is "We were bored after two weeks and went to London to spend a few days before our departure for home." This paraphrase keeps the meaning of the original.

____

____

____

____

____

____

____

____

____

Analyze each of the three sections circled in blue that you have selected in step 2 to determine if the order of information changed the meaning. Describe how the differences in order of information changed the meaning. For example, Ella's sentence is "However, after about two weeks in Sheffield we got bored and decided to go to London for few days before we had to go home." My paraphrase is "We were bored and decided to go to London." This keeps the same order of information but is not accurate because information is left out. In the paraphrase "A few days before we had to go home, we decided to go to London because after two weeks in Sheffield, we were bored," the order of information is changed but the meaning is not affected, so this is an acceptable paraphrase.

____

____

____

____

Step 4   Assessment

Review your work in steps 2 and 3 and determine if you are able to accurately paraphrase propositions that occur in running discourse. If you are not sure, then go to the original sentences and replace the words one at a time with synonyms. Try using passive voice or active voice to help you create paraphrases that do not change the meaning. Write a description of how your awareness of the importance of accuracy in paraphrasing has changed as a result of doing this exercise.

____

____

____

____

Step 5   **Action**

You can take further action to improve your paraphrasing skills by selecting the remaining parts of the transcript for deeper analysis and revision, following the steps in the study questions and follow-up. Another suggestion for action is to play the videotape again and pause it at every second beep tone instead of every beep tone and paraphrase what you have heard. A third suggestion is to repeat this process with another selection from this videotape.

EXERCISE 5.2

My Life Story
ED PERKIN

See directions for the teacher in Exercise 5.1

Directions

Student Workbook
page 167

You will do this exercise first in workbook mode and then real-time. Then do the study questions and follow-up. You will need a tape recorder and blank tape for your recorder and a red, blue, and black pen or pencil for this exercise.

Workbook Paraphrasing

Begin with workbook paraphrasing. A written transcript shows the speaker's words. Refer to the transcript. Read it from start to finish one time and then turn on your recording device and paraphrase the information, one sentence at a time. Pause between sentences. Keep the features of a good paraphrase in mind. Avoid repeating the selection word for word. A word-for-word repetition is not the same as a paraphrase. Transcribe your paraphrases in the space provided.

Transcript for *My Life Story,* by Ed Perkin

1.   My name is Ed Perkin. I was born on January 9, 1972, to two British people, uh, who were living in South Africa at the time.

Workbook	*I'm Ed Perkin and my birthdate is January 9, 1972. My parents are both British*

and were living in South Africa when I was born.

Real-time

2.	They were there on business so I was born in Johannesburg, South Africa. I lived there for nine months before my parents returned to England, where I, uh, grew up.

Workbook	*I was born in Johannesburg, South Africa, while my parents were there on*

business. Nine months after I was born my parents returned to England,

which is where I grew up.

Real-time

3.	Uh, I lived in England and went, uh, to school for my first couple of years at school, uh, 'til about age 7 and then we came to America.

Workbook	*When I was about seven, we came to America. Before that I went to school in*

England for the first few years of school.

Real-time

4.	Uh, my father, uh, decided he wanted to live in Houston because at that time (in the late seventies) that was the boom town because of all the oil business.

Workbook   *In the late seventies my father decided he wanted to live in Houston because it*

                  was an important city in the oil business then.

Real-time   ____

                  ____

5.   And, um, we lived there for about three years before we moved out here to
      San Diego.

Workbook   *We moved to San Diego after living in Houston for about three years.*

                  ____

Real-time   ____

                  ____

6.   And we've been living in San Diego ever since, uh, with the exception of
      when I went to college.

Workbook   *Except for the time during college, I have lived in San Diego ever since.*

                  ____

Real-time   ____

                  ____

7.   I think that my life has been affected quite a bit by all this moving around
      because I never really spent more than about two years at any one school.

Workbook   *I never spent more than two years in any school, so I think that all the moving*

                  around has affected my life quite alot.

Real-time   ____

                  ____

8.   Uh, I spent about two years (as I said) in England.

Workbook   *As I said, I spent about two years in England.*

Real-time

9.   Then we moved to Houston, where I spent one year at one school and we moved across town so I attended another elementary school for about a year and a half.

Workbook   *While in Houston, I attended two elementary schools. I attended the first one for about a year and the second for about 18 months.*

Real-time

10.   Uh, at that point we came to San Diego. I was in the fifth grade at that time, and I spent all of the fifth grade and most of the sixth grade at a, uh, school in Scripps Ranch, which is a suburb of San Diego.

Workbook   *When I was in fifth grade, we moved to San Diego and I attended a school in a suburb of San Diego, Scripps Ranch, for fifth and most of sixth grades.*

Real-time

11.   And then I moved to uh, Rancho Bernardo (which is another suburb), where I attended a different, uh, school. That was a middle school, so I made the leap from elementary to middle school, uh, at the same time that I went to a new school; so that was an interesting experience.

Workbook   *Then I attended a different school in Rancho Bernardo, where we moved next. I*

went from elementary to middle school when I transferred to the new school,

which was interesting.

Real-time

12.   And I was there for slightly over two years before I went to high school.

Workbook   *I was at that new school until I went to high school two years later.*

Real-time

13.   My parents then decided it was time to move again, so we moved across
town where I attended a different high school, and I was there for my last
two years (my junior year and senior year of high school) before going to
college.

Workbook   *My parents next decision was to move across town and there I attended a different*

high school for my last two years of high school before going to college.

Real-time

14. So college was really the first time that I spent a full four years at any one school, and I find that I've made most of the friends that I have now at college, probably for that reason.

Workbook *Most of the friends I have now, I made while I was in college and that is probably*

because that was the first time I was in one school for four years.

Real-time

Real-Time Paraphrasing

Real-time paraphrasing is the second part of this exercise. Find this selection on your tape. Turn on your recording device and listen to the selection again until you hear the first beep tone on the videotape. Stop the videotape and record your paraphrase on your tape recorder. Repeat this process until you reach the end of the video selection. Remember to use all the features of a good paraphrase as discussed in Unit 4 and this unit. Stop the videotape and your recording device at the end of this selection.

Study Questions

1. Read your workbook paraphrase and compare the transcript of the original sentences to your workbook paraphrase. Does your paraphrase convey the same meaning as the original?

2. Transcribe your real-time paraphrase. If your paraphrase does not convey the same meaning as the original, use red to circle those parts of the transcript that are skewed in your real-time paraphrase. Is the information in the same order? Use blue to circle information that is correct but is presented in a different order in your paraphrase than in the original. Use black to underline where you added information that was not in the original.

3. Reexamine both versions of your paraphrase and make a list of the order of events as you conveyed them. Use the blue circles in your answer to question 2 to help you with this. Compare these lists with each other. Are they the same? Compare these with the original to see if the order of information is the same. Sometimes the order of events can be altered slightly without changing the meaning. Would it change the message if you changed the order of events?

<table>
<tr><th>Workbook</th><th>Real-time</th></tr>
</table>

4. Check for question forms in the source and in your workbook and real-time paraphrases. Are there any instances where using a question form would be better? If so, put a red question mark on the transcript at that location. Are there places where you used a question form that altered the meaning? If so, put a blue question mark on the transcript at that location.

5. Check the spoken, original text, and both versions of your paraphrase for idiomatic expressions. List any idiomatic expressions that you found in the original text. Did you paraphrase the idioms or repeat the idiomatic expressions? If you repeated any idiomatic expressions instead of paraphrasing them, write out the meaning of the idioms here.

____

____

____

____

Five-Step Follow-up

Step 1   Observation

Review your answers and make sure you complete all parts of the exercise.

Step 2   Selection

Select the portions that you circled in red in question 2. These are the parts of your paraphrases that do not have the same meaning as the original sentence. Choose a total of three examples from your real-time paraphrase to analyze.

Select the portions that you circled in blue in question 2. These are the parts of your paraphrase that do not have the same order of information as the original sentence. Choose a total of three examples from your real-time paraphrase to analyze.

Step 3   Analysis

Using the three selections that you have circled in step 2, determine which part of the form of the paraphrase changes the meaning. Redo the paraphrase so that the original meaning is preserved.

____

____

____

____

____

____

Analyze each of the three sections circled in blue that you selected in step 2B to determine if the order of information changed the meaning. Describe how the difference in order changed the meaning.

____

____

____

____

Step 4   Assessment

Review your work in steps 2 and 3 and determine if you are able to accurately paraphrase propositions that occur in running discourse. If you are not sure, then go to the original sentences and replace the words one at a time with synonyms. Try using passive voice or active voice to help you create paraphrases that do not change the meaning. Write a description of how your awareness of the importance of accuracy in paraphrasing has changed as a result of doing this exercise.

____

____

____

Step 5   Action

You can take further action to improve your paraphrasing skills by selecting the remaining parts of the transcript for deeper analysis and revision, following the steps in the study questions and follow-up. Another suggestion for action is to play the videotape again and pause it at every second beep tone instead of every beep tone and paraphrase what you have heard. A third suggestion is to repeat this process with another selection from this videotape.

My Early Years
THYRA BENOIT

Directions

Student Workbook
page 176

You will do this exercise first in workbook mode and then real-time. Then do the study questions and the follow-up. You will need a tape recorder and blank tape for your recorder and a red, blue, and black pen or pencil for this exercise.

Workbook Paraphrasing

Begin with workbook paraphrasing. A written transcript shows the speaker's words. Refer to the transcript. Read it from start to finish one time and then turn on your recording device and paraphrase the information, one sentence at a time. Pause between sentences. Keep the features of a good paraphrase in mind. Avoid repeating the selection word for word. A word-for-word repetition is not the same as a paraphrase. Transcribe your paraphrases in the space provided.

Transcript for *My Early Years,* by Thyra Benoit

1. I'm Thyra Benoit: T-h-y-r-a B-e-n-o-i-t. This is part one of my story.

Workbook   *My name is Thyra Benoit. This is how my story starts.*

Real-time

2. I was born in Washington in the great year of 1950. However, due to family difficulties my parents divorced and I moved to Watertown, Massachusetts.

Workbook   *In 1950, I was born in Washington DC. That was a good year. My parents*

divorced due to family problems and after that I lived in Watertown,

Massachusetts.

Real-time

3.   Some of you may know Watertown, as it is the home of the Perkins School
     for the Blind and the Deaf.

Workbook   *Watertown is where the Perkins School for the Blind and Deaf is located, which is*

why some of you may know Watertown.

Real-time

4.   It wasn't until I started college in 1968 that I realized that people don't cross
     streets with bells. Can you imagine what it was like going to school in
     Boston (I attended Simmons College) and trying to cross the street with red
     and yellow lights flashing at the same time and hearing no bells and almost
     getting hit by a car?

Workbook   *Until I went to college, I thought everyone relied on sound, such as bells, to help*

them cross the street. When I went to Simmons College in Boston that was the

first time I had to cross the street using lights, not bells, and I nearly got hit

by a car.

Real-time

5.   Well anyway, that was my big adventure about going to school
     in Boston.

Workbook   *So going to school in Boston was a big adventure for me.*

Real-time

6.   At Simmons College I started as a nursing/physical therapy major, but I
     decided that if I wanted to graduate on time I would be better off majoring
     in something else,

Workbook   *At first I was a nursing/physical therapy major when I went to Simmons College.*

 Then I decided that I would be able to graduate in less time by majoring in

 something else.

Real-time

7.   so I chose French. I liked languages and I liked to mimic people. In any
     case, then I had to decide what to do.

Workbook   *I had to decide what to do next, so I changed to a major in French because I liked*

 languages and could imitate people.

Real-time

8.   I thought, well maybe I would major in French and then go on and become a social worker.

Workbook   *I thought I'd go on to become a social worker after majoring in French.*

Real-time

9.   But first I had to get through college, so I also took education classes.

Workbook   *I took education classes in order to get through college.*

Real-time

10.   And I had the pleasure of teaching on the high school level at an experimental school. Can you imagine what it's like to be in a class with the students being permitted to literally hang out of the window? Well that was acceptable.

Workbook   *Can you picture what it is like to teach a class of high school students who were permitted to hang out the windows? Well that was perfectly OK in the school I taught at, which was an experimental school*

Real-time

11.   I got through the year and then I left Boston and came to Washington, DC, where I attended Howard University School of Social Work.

Workbook   *I left Boston after getting through that year and moved to Washington, DC. There, I attended the School of Social Work at Howard University.*

Real-time

12.   I was in an experimental class, and it seems like all of my academic years have been filled with experiments or first-timers.

Workbook   *It seems as though all of my academic years have been filled with experimental or first-time situations. The class I was in was also experimental.*

Real-time

13.   When I started school in Boston they got away–they did away with grades.

Workbook   *They did away with grades when I started school in Boston.*

Real-time

14.   And I don't know if any of you have had that experience, but it permits you to be very focused on what interests you, where you can give your talents, and on the mandatory subjects which don't necessarily meet your academic needs, you can get by.

Workbook   *Having no grades allows you to really focus on what interests you, where your*

talents lie. On the required subjects, which you might be less interested in, you

can just do the minimum. I am not sure if any of you have had that kind

of experience.

Real-time

15.   Well anyway, Simmons was wonderful, I came to Howard and I
learned I was in a new "thrust" class. And that meant we went straight
through a two-year program, we finished in a year and a half, with no
grades again.

Workbook   *In any case, I thought Simmons was wonderful. When I got to Howard, I was in a*

two-year, nongraded program, which was a new "thrust." That means that we

completed a two-year program in 18 months.

Real-time

16.   So, I'm here in Washington and I'm here to stay. And I thoroughly enjoyed
my experience at Howard; it is where I met Dr. Marquessa Brown, and it is
through my friendship with her that I stand before you today. Thank you.

Workbook   *When I was at Howard, which I really liked, I met Dr. Marquessa Brown, and*

                      through that friend, I have been able to come and give this speech to you

                      today. I'm here in Washington and here to stay.

Real-time   ____

                      ____

                      ____

Real-Time Paraphrasing

Real-time paraphrasing is the second part of this exercise. Find this selection on your tape. Turn on your recording device and listen until you hear the first beep tone on the videotape. Stop the tape and record your paraphrase on your tape recorder. Repeat this process until you reach the end of the video selection. Remember to use all the features of a good paraphrase as discussed in Unit 4 and this unit. Stop the videotape and your recording device at the end of this selection.

Study Questions

1. Read the first copy of the transcript at the end of the study questions. Read your workbook paraphrase and compare the transcript of the original sentences to your workbook paraphrase. Does your paraphrase convey the same meaning as the original?

   ____

   ____

   ____

   ____

2. Transcribe your real-time paraphrase. If your paraphrase does not convey the same meaning as the original, use red to circle those parts of the transcript that are skewed in your real-time paraphrase. Is the information in the same order? Use blue to circle information that is correct but is presented in a different order in your paraphrase than in the original. Use black to underline where you added information that was not in the original.

3. Reexamine both versions of your paraphrase and make a list of the order
    of events as you conveyed them. Use the blue circles in your answer to
    question 2 to help you with this. Compare these lists with each other. Are
    they the same? Compare these with the original to see if the order of in-
    formation is the same. Sometimes the order of events can be altered
    slightly without changing the meaning. Would it change the message if
    you changed the order of events?

Workbook	Real-time
__________	__________
__________	__________
__________	__________
__________	__________
__________	__________
__________	__________
__________	__________
__________	__________
__________	__________
__________	__________
__________	__________
__________	__________
__________	__________
__________	__________

_______________________________   _______________________________

_______________________________   _______________________________

4. Check for question forms in the source and in your workbook and real-time paraphrases. Would using a question form improve your paraphrases? If so, put a red question mark on the transcript at that location. Are there places where you use a question form that alters the meaning? If so, put a blue question mark on the transcript at that location.

5. Check the spoken, original text, and both versions of your paraphrase for idiomatic expressions. List any idiomatic expressions that you found in the original text. Did you paraphrase the idioms or repeat the idiomatic expressions? If so, put a blue question mark on the transcript at that location. If you repeated any idiomatic expressions instead of paraphrasing them, write out the meaning of the idioms here.

____

____

____

____

Five-Step Follow-up

Step I   Observation

Review your answers and make sure you complete all parts of the exercise.

Step 2   Selection

Select the portions that you circled in red in question 2. These are the parts of your paraphrases that do not have the same meaning as the original sentence. Choose a total of three examples from your real-time paraphrase to analyze.

Select the portions that you circled in blue in question 2. These are the parts of your paraphrase that do not have the same order of information as the original sentence. Choose a total of three examples from your real-time paraphrase to analyze.

Step 3   Analysis

Using the three selections that you have circled in step 2, determine which part of the form of the paraphrase changes the meaning. Redo the paraphrase so that the original meaning is preserved.

Analyze each of the three sections circled in blue that you selected in step 2B to determine if the order of information changed the meaning. Describe how the difference in order changed the meaning.

Step 4   Assessment

Review your work in steps 2 and 3 and determine if you are able to accurately paraphrase propositions that occur in running discourse. If you are not sure, then go to the original sentences and replace the words one at a time with synonyms. Try using passive voice or active voice to help you create paraphrases that do not change the meaning. Write a description of how your awareness of the importance of accuracy in paraphrasing has changed as a result of doing this exercise.

Step 5   Action

You can take further action to improve your paraphrasing skills by selecting the remaining parts of the transcript for deeper analysis and revision, following the steps in the study questions and follow-up. Another suggestion for action is to play the videotape again and pause it at every second beep tone instead of every beep tone and paraphrase what you have heard. A third suggestion is to repeat this process with another selection from this videotape.

Additional Exercises

Refer to the video selections from Unit 4. Paraphrase the entire story, as a unit, not sentence by sentence, without shortening or lengthening it and without changing the meaning. Turn on your recording device to record your work. Check your paraphrase to see that the meaning has been preserved and that you have presented the information in the same order that the speaker used.

Progress Tracking Sheet

This sheet is designed to help you keep track of which exercises you have completed and how well you have done on these exercises. See page 13 (Teacher's Guide page 20) for a full description of how to use the Progress Tracking Sheet.

Exercise Number	Date	First Performance	Study Questions	Follow-up Activity	Questions and Reminders	Date	Second Performance
Exercise 5.1 Quantitative							
Qualitative							
Exercise 5.2 Quantitative							
Qualitative							
Exercise 5.3 Quantitative							
Qualitative							
Quantitative Totals							

UNIT 6

Main Idea Identification

Introduction

In this unit the emphasis is on comprehension of the most important points in spoken discourse. Direct practice in this skill for interpreters is often overlooked, as are many direct exercises in English improvement. Comprehension of spoken material is an important aspect of intralingual skill proficiency. Strong comprehension skills improve your ability to find the most important parts of spoken discourse. Interpreters need to make quick decisions about which points are main ideas and which points support the main idea, so this unit provides practice in finding the main idea and key words that point to the main idea. This unit introduces the concept of schema and shows how understanding schemas can help the interpreter find the main point.

In order to identify the main idea, you must sort the ideas by level of importance and then by topic. This is accomplished using a specific type of analytical thinking called hierarchical thinking. A hierarchy is a rank ordering or arranging of things in order of importance.

In a well-organized speech or talk, the main idea usually is expressed early in the speech or text. The main idea can be summarized into a topic sentence, which is sometimes further abbreviated into a title. The main idea is stated early in the speech and then referred to again and again until the topic is changed. Once the main idea is stated, it becomes implicit or understood in the ideas that follow it. Ideas presented after the main idea can be points that clarify or support the main idea.

Topics included in this unit are main idea, key word, and schema.

Main Idea

In this unit the term main idea means the central premise around which the rest of the speech is expanded. The supporting ideas are those that help expand the main idea. If the main idea is altered or deleted, the meaning of the text changes. The main idea contains important information. Supporting ideas add information to the main idea and make it clearer and stronger. The supporting ideas or details are less important to the overall theme than the main point. If supporting ideas are omitted, the overall main idea is not changed substantially.

You may remember reading classes in which you learned to find the main idea. The goal of finding the main idea usually is to improve or check on comprehension. Cunningham and Moore (1986) searched the literature on main idea comprehension and found that there are many terms that refer to the concept of main idea. Some of the terms associated with main idea include outstanding point, master idea, big idea, controlling idea, significant idea, and central theme. Even among professionals in the field of reading for comprehension, there is not much agreement on how to define the term main idea. Despite disagreements regarding the definition of the term, it is true that there are ideas in any passage or text that are more important than other ideas or are more central to the overall theme. Working to develop this distinction between more important and less important ideas is the goal of this unit.

Cunningham and Moore (1986) suggest that one of the factors that determine what a person selects as the main idea is what captures their attention. These authors deal primarily with finding the main idea in written materials, rather than spoken, but the same principles apply to finding the main point of spoken and written material. Cunningham and Moore write, "The reader's purposes for reading as well as writer's presentation of information serve to regulate reader's attention" (1986, p. 10). If we expand the concept of "the reader" to include the interpreter, we can see that it is important to say that the interpreter's purpose in listening is to extract as much meaning as possible from the passage and convey it into the target language. The interpreter is not listening to gain information for his or her own personal use and so may focus more on the speaker's purpose. However, as Cunningham and Moore point out, the writer's or speaker's purpose may not always be easy to find.

Key Word

"The key word in a passage is the one that labels the most important single concept in a passage" (Cunningham and Moore, 1986). According to Larson (1984, p.177), "Key words are used over and over in the text and are crucial to the theme or topic under discussion. Key words are most often words which represent an essential or basic concept of the text and are often thematic." Key words point to the main idea. Learning to identify key words is an effective way to improve comprehension.

Schema

A schema, or frame of reference, is a plan or diagram. Speakers who wish to convey information generally have a schema for that information and ideas about which parts of the information are most central to the message. This means that the speaker usually has a plan for what they want to say. In addition, the concept of schema includes what the speaker already knows about the topic. It can be thought of as the speaker's prior history and experience with that topic. For example, a teacher giving a lecture on aerodynamics may have personal experiences with this topic as well as information obtained through study.

There can be many different schemas in any communicative event. For example, if you are a student, you have a schema for a lecture class and a different one for a lab class. Your schema for a lecture class is like a mental pattern for what you expect in a lecture class. You have a different mental pattern for what you expect in a lab class. Schemas are usually based on real-world experiences. Sometimes it is possible to create a schema for something you have never seen or experienced, but usually that schema draws on schemas for similar or related experiences that you have had before. The most important point is that schemas are very personal and no two people will have exactly the same schema, even for shared events. There is enough overlap, however, that knowing that you must tap into a schema will help you because the schema provides a framework within which to organize the ideas.

Each speaker has his or her own schemas for the topic at hand. This crucial piece of information is usually not explicitly discussed when, and if, the speaker meets with the interpreter prior to beginning the speech, meeting, or class. For example, it is unlikely that the speaker will explain their schema to the interpreter. Rather, the speaker may disclose some of the details about the content of the speech at hand, and not what the speaker has known about this topic and how this speech fits into the speaker's overall scheme of things.

At the same time, the interpreter brings his or her own schema or frame of reference to any communicative event. Since interpreter's work is often in varied fields of information other than the field of interpretation, the frame of reference of the interpreter could possibly be the weakest of any of the participants in the communicative event. As Gile (1995) points out, interpreters rarely interpret about interpreting.

The audience member or members will also have their own frame of reference. Naturally, the interpreter cannot know all that influences the audience, but it is helpful to realize that each person brings their own frame of reference to the communicative event. Knowing that your schema may be different than those of the people you are working with can allow you the freedom to ask questions if you are not sure what is meant.

The Role of Comprehension through Main Idea Identification in the Interpretation Process

The simultaneous interpreter must quickly grasp the important parts of the speaker's message. To render a faithful interpretation, the interpreter must sort out the main ideas from the supporting ideas. This usually happens without benefit of a discussion of this distinction with the speaker. In the speaker's mind and perhaps in the speaker's notes, some points are more important than others. If the interpreter attributes equal weight to all of the speaker's points, the message may be skewed and certainly will not match the speaker's original message.

Sometimes, the speaker speaks very rapidly or is reading from a prepared speech. In these cases, the interpreter cannot always ask the speaker to pause or repeat information. When this happens, it is important for the interpreter to select the most important points. The ideal interpretation includes all of the main points and all of the supporting points, in the order originally presented. In real-world practice, this is not always possible. In situations in which the interpreter is unable to slow the pace of the speaker's comments, it is necessary for the interpreter to select which points are central and which are supporting.

This skill of finding the main idea is one that is used in the real world and in interpreter education. Various authors write about the importance of this skill. Ine VanDam (1989) describes a process she calls "Hop, Skip and Jump." By this she means that when the interpreter cannot keep up with the pace of the speaker, the interpreter must hop and skip over some of the details and jump to the next main point. In order to do this, the interpreter must be able to discern which points are central and which are supporting.

The following exercises are designed to provide opportunities to improve comprehension by practicing listening to natural spoken English.

Discussion Questions

Discuss the following questions with your students to promote insight and increase awareness of the importance of main idea comprehension as it relates to the interpretation process.

1. *How does understanding the importance of main idea identification in English relate to the interpretation process?*

    Interpreters must be able to quickly sift through the streams of incoming material to find the central organizing points. When the interpreter grasps which ideas are most central, the interpreter can better sort the remaining information into details and supporting facts.

    The ability to quickly find the "gist" is sometimes used to determine suitability for interpreter training. Finding the gist is central to the interpretation process.

If the student cannot easily find the gist of the message, this may point to the fact that another profession may be a better match for that student's skills and abilities.

2. *Do you feel you have good main idea comprehension skills?*

   Ask this question before and after the drills to see if students say their skills improved and if they have greater confidence in them. Most students' comprehension skills will improve with increased focus and practice. Confidence in the ability to find the main idea quickly benefits the interpreter. Rapid and reliable main idea identification drills are not automatic. These skills must be learned and practiced. Even though students think that they have accurate and reliable main idea identification skills, it is often the case that these skills need improvement.

3. *What will happen if the interpreter does not have rapid, reliable main idea identification skills?*

   When the interpreter does not have quick access to main idea identification skills, not only is the richness of the product of the interpretation compromised, but also the interpretation process is weakened. For example, the interpreter who cannot identify the main idea gets lost in the details and often misses the central point of the text.

4. *What happens when the interpreter does not know which ideas are main and which are supporting?*

   In this case the interpreter will not be able to sort out which ideas are the main ideas and will not be able to organize the supporting ideas around the main idea. When the interpreter cannot rank ideas in order of importance, all of the incoming information has the same level of importance and soon the interpreter's cognitive processing capacity will be reached or exceeded. The mind can function better if it can group relevant ideas together and distinguish ideas that are dissimilar. The result of the interpretation, in the event that the interpreter can keep going, may be a series of individually translated items without grasp of the big picture the speaker wishes to convey.

Main Idea Identification Exercises

Decide if you want to conduct these exercises in class, or if you want the students to do them on their own time. The exercises can easily be done in a group format. In this case you will need to decide if the students can write while listening or should respond only after having listened to the entire selection.

Finding the main point without taking notes while listening is more difficult than finding the main point while taking notes. Choose the level of difficulty that is appropriate for your students.

Take time to go over the directions for each section, workbook and real-time. Read the directions and explain them to the students. Allow time for questions after you have given the directions. You should plan at least five minutes to prepare the students for the exercise. Five minutes should be enough, if you have the group's attention, and if all equipment is ready and in working order. All tapes needed for these exercises must be cued to the correct spot.

EXERCISE 6.1

How to Operate a Swimming Pool
ED PERKIN

Directions

Student Workbook
page 191

Find this selection on your tape. Adjust the volume as necessary. Begin by allowing yourself time to focus on the speaker's face. This video selection is about five minutes long. Answer the study questions and do the follow-up. You will need a red, blue, and black pen or pencil for this exercise.

Study Questions

1. What is the speaker's purpose in giving this speech? Is the purpose stated or implied? How do you know? Write your answer in complete sentences.

   The speaker's purpose is to give instructions for managing the filtration and

   pumping system in a back yard swimming pool that has a spa attached.

   The speaker often states his or her intended purpose at the beginning of

   the lecture. It is not always the case that the stated purpose will lead to

   discovery of the main idea, but it is likely to. Sometimes the title is also

   the main idea of the speech. In this case the author created the title after

   the speech. The title was not created by the speaker.

2. What is the speech about? Write your answer in a single complete sentence. Write as many key words as you can remember from this speech.

____

____

____

____

The speech is Ed's explanation of how to operate and care for the pool and spa in his parent's backyard.

Keywords: pool, spa, waterfall, pump, heater, valve, drain, return, suction, circulate.

These key words are used repeatedly and point toward the most important ideas in the speech.

3. What is the speaker's schema or frame of reference? Why do you think so?

____

____

____

____

His frame of reference is that he knows from experience how to manage the pool pump and filtration system. He said he has become the person responsible for knowing how to operate it and so we infer that he knows how to operate it correctly.

4. Listen to the selection again. While listening list the main points and list the supporting points below the main point.

◆ *Pool operation can be difficult.* _______________________________

• *The pool and spa take a lot of work and Ed is the one in his family*

that takes care of them. __________________________________

◆ *It is important to know how to correctly operate the heater for the spa and pool.*

   • *The heater is not needed for the pool, but is used for the spa when they have parties.*

◆ *The drain and return systems for the spa need to be set in such a way as to operate as one system.*

   • *The specific operation of the valves.*

◆ *You would use other settings if you wanted to do different things with the water in the pool or spa.*

   • *The specific steps in turning on the pump.*

◆ *You need to follow specific steps to turn on the spa heater, and to turn it off you use the same steps in reverse.*

   • *How to regulate the heat.*

   • *Turning off the heater is a specific procedure—these steps are supporting points.*

   • *The reasons why you must be careful in turning off the heater.*

____

____

____

____

____

____

____

____

____

____

____

____

____

5. Read the transcript. Circle key words in black. Look for main ideas and supporting ideas. Circle the main ideas in the transcript in red and underline the supporting ideas in red. Compare the transcript to the list you made in study question 4. Did you select the same main and supporting ideas when you listened to the tape the first and second time? Key words point to the main idea. If there are main ideas in your list that are not in the transcript, circle them in blue. If there are main ideas in the transcript that are not in your list, circle them twice in red.

    There should not be much discrepancy between the list of main and supporting points and the items that are circled in this answer.

Transcript for *How to Operate a Swimming Pool,* by Ed Perkin

1   My name is Ed Perkin and I am going to discuss how you operate

2   the, uh, the pool at my parents' house. Uh, they have a, uh, pool

3   which has a over—uh, overhead spa, if you will, and a waterfall that

4   runs alongside it. Uh, it's very nice to look at but it takes a lot of

5   work, and, uh, somehow I have become the one who's the expert at

6   doing this. So, uh, I'm left with the responsibility of knowing all the

7   little ins and outs of the pump and the waterfall and the lights and

8   the—everything that goes with it.

9   Um, mainly—the main thing that's difficult to do, I suppose, and

10   that sort of encapsulates everything that you need to know about

11   operating the pool is when you want to have the heater on on either

12   the pool or the spa. Uh, we don't really use the heater for the pool

13   because we live in San Diego where it's warm most of the year 'round,

14   and no one really wants to go swimming in December anyway. So we

15   usually only use the heater for the spa when we have guests over, or a

16   party or something of that sort. Uh, the first thing that you need to

17   do is there's two valves: one drains either the pool or the spa; the

18   other valve returns the water to the pool or spa. So if you want to

19   heat the—the spa you need to have it set on draining the spa and

20   returning the water to the spa so that it is all one system, and you

21   leave the water in the pool sagnan—stagnant for the time being. Uh,

22   vice versa if you want to heat the pool you would set it on pool

23   suction (as it's called) and pool return. Uh, if you wanted to run the

24   water so that it flowed out of the spa and into the pool, giving a—a

25   waterfall sort of effect, you would put it on pool suction–spa return

26   so the water returns into the spa and flows over the edge into the

27   pool. If you wanted to drain the spa for cleaning purposes you would

28   put it on spa suction–pool return.

29　　　Uh, so first you need to put it on (as I said) spa suction–spa

30　　return and then turn the pump on. This will get the water circulating.

31　　Next you, uh, turn the heater on. That's located in the large box to

32　　the, uh, side. Uh, it's a switch on the side and there's also a dial there

33　　which can turn the heat either up or down, but you should be careful

34　　because if you turn the heat too low the pilot light will go off and

35　　then you'll just have gas running through without any heat. Uh, right

36　　now the pilot light is on. It wasn't working last year, but everything

37　　seems to be fine. So you (again) put it on spa suction–spa return,

38　　turn the pump on, put the heater on, and in about an hour you'll

39　　have some nice warm water to sit in.

40　　　Uh, turning it off is a little more important because you can't

41　　really mess things up when you turn it on, but when you turn it off

42　　there's a—a crucial mistake which is possible if you're not careful.

43　　The, uh—basically you want to do everything backwards. The first

44　　thing you do is you turn the heater off. But now—and this is the

45　　important part—you must wait at least fifteen minutes before shutting

46　　the pump down. The reason for this is if you don't shut the pump

47　　down and you have the heater off—uh, or rather, even if you had the

48　　heater on—if you shut the pump off the water will stop circulating

49　　and, uh, one amount of water will sit next to the heater and it will be

50　　caused to overheat. So it is very important that you let the water

51　　circulate after you've turned the heater off so that it can cool down

52　　naturally. Uh, the other mistake is if you switch off of the spoo—

53　　excuse me—the spa suction–spa return and you put it on, say, spa

54　　suction–pool return, then you would, uh, or rather, pool suction–spa

55　　return, you would then bring cool water into the system and this

56　　would—this would run past the very hot heater and it could crack.

57　　So it's very important to switch the heater off, wait fifteen minutes,

58　　then turn the pump off before messing with the valves again.

Five-Step Follow-up

Step 1   Observation

Review your answers to the study questions and be sure you have answered all parts.

Step 2   Selection

Refer to the blue circles from your answer to study question 5. These are ideas that you listed as main ideas, but were not in the transcript. Refer to the portions of the transcript that have double red circles. These are the main ideas that you did not detect until you read the transcript. Be prepared to analyze these portions in step 3.

This selection process will help focus on important points that were missed. This exercise helps to isolate specific areas where the main point was not accurately identified in the first contact with the selection.

Step 3   Analysis

Analyze for accuracy. In group discussion, compare answers to study question 1. What is the speaker's purpose in giving this speech? Through discussion, see if the group can arrive at consensus regarding the purpose of the speech and if it is stated or implied. If you missed any of the main points, decide what contributed to your missing the importance of the points.

____

____

____

____

The title of a speech may or may not reflect the main point. In this case the titles are as reflective of the main points as possible. The purpose of the speech is why a speech is given and includes main and supporting points to convey the ideas.

Using the responses to follow-up question 2, choose two ideas that you listed as main ideas that were not in the transcript. Choose two ideas that were main ideas in the transcript that did not appear in your list. Why did the main ideas not appear in your list?

____

____

____

____

Students may miss main points if they are not yet able to arrange ideas in order of importance. If this occurs, then you may want to assign drills and practice in outlining. Outlining any of the speeches on this tape or other material you select will help students see which ideas are central and which are supporting. Central ideas cannot be deleted while some details can be without adversely affecting the overall main idea.

Step 4   Assessment

If you had more than two places on the transcript that had double red circles it may mean that you are missing main points as you listen. Write down the number of instances of double red circles here. if you have no double red circles then you are making good progress.

____

Step 5   Action

Develop a plan for action based on your analysis and assessment. Listen to the passage again and mentally note when the speaker states one of the important points and when he states supporting points. Make a mental outline of these points as a way to practice sorting and ranking ideas as you hear them.

You can suggest other materials for students to practice outlining. For example, selections from other exercises in this workbook and video are appropriate for comprehension exercises.

EXERCISE 6.2

Environmental Changes
RICHARD SOMERVILLE

Directions

Student Workbook
page 198

The video selection is approximately eight minutes long. Find this selection on your tape. Adjust the volume as necessary. Begin by allowing yourself time to focus on the speaker's face. Listen to this selection. Do not write while listening. Do not read the transcript yet. Stop the tape at the end of this selection and answer the study questions and then do the follow-up exercise. You need a red, blue, and black pen or pencil for this exercise.

Study Questions

1. What is the speaker's purpose in giving this speech? Is the purpose stated or implied? How do you know? Write your answer in complete sentences.

    The speaker's purpose in giving the speech is to inform an unseen audience

    about the ozone hole and greenhouse effect. He gave the speech in

    response to the author's request for a videotaped lecture that could be used

    in interpreter training. He states his purpose in the first line of his speech.

2. What is the speech about? Write your answer as a single complete sentence. Write as many key words as you can remember from this speech.

    The speech explains how people's habits affect the atmosphere in at least two

    important ways, resulting in "the ozone hole" and the "greenhouse effect."

    Key words: environment, ozone, stratosphere, chemicals, atmosphere, earth,

    freons (chloroflurocarbons), greenhouse effect, carbon dioxide, climate,

    fossil fuels, political action.

3. What is the speaker's schema or frame of reference? Explain your reasoning.

The speaker appears to be very knowledgeable about this topic. This

impression is based on this speech alone. He has presented a complicated

topic in a short, well-organized speech. In fact he works for Scripps

Oceanographic Institute, in San Diego, California.

4. Listen to the selection again. While listening write the main points and list supporting points below the main points.

◆ *Environmental changes can affect the planet and can be caused by*

people's actions.

◆ *One of the environmental changes is the ozone hole.*

  • *Ozone gas occurs naturally in the atmosphere.*

◆ *Chemical usage was the primary cause of the ozone hole.*

  • *Two scientist in the 1970s thought that the ozone hole might be caused*

  by the use of freons.

  • *Other scientists ten years later discovered that the ozone in Antarctica*

  was disappearing and replenishing each year.

◆ *Political action stopped the use of these dangerous chemicals.*

  • *The discovery of the ozone hole was a surprise and led to*

  legislation that prevents the use of freons in the United States and

  soon everywhere.

◆ *Over time, ozone levels are expected to return to natural levels again*

◆ *The greenhouse effect is the second environmental change and is more complicated.*

◆ *We need the greenhouse effect to support life on earth.*

  • *The greenhouse effect is a natural effect created from chemicals like carbon dioxide and methane that trap heat so it can't escape from the earth's surface.*

  • *If we did not have the greenhouse effect we would have a cold climate like the moon.*

◆ *The people on Earth use fossil fuels to a large extent and this usage has magnified the greenhouse effect.*

  • *There are over 6 billion people on earth now and the number is growing rapidly.*

  • *These people use fossil fuels like coal, oil, and natural gas to generate energy.*

  • *These fuels generate carbon monoxide, which affects the greenhouse effect.*

◆ *The increased greenhouse effect results in global warming, which in turn can lead to climate change.*

  • *Scientists are not sure how serious the increased greenhouse effect is, but think that in the 21st century Earth will be 3 to 5° warmer than it is now.*

  • *Sea level will rise due to increased melting of glaciers.*

  • *Higher sea levels will change storm patterns.*

◆ *People can influence environmental changes as much as nature can.*

• *Most of these changes will adversely affect climate.*

• *It will be difficult to alter human behavior to protect the climate because there are so many people and they use so much energy.*

• *Much research is needed to understand climate change, what affects it, and what political action can help solve the problem.*

• *The ozone hole is a symbol which shows how people can make a difference if they work together to save the environment.*

____

____

____

____

____

____

____

____

____

5. Read the transcript. Circle key words in black. Look for main ideas and supporting ideas. Circle the main ideas in the transcript in red and underline the supporting ideas in red. Compare the transcript to the list you made in study question 4. Did you select the same main and supporting ideas as you listened to the tape the first and second time? If there are main ideas in your list that are not in the transcript, circle them in blue. If there are main ideas in the transcript that are not in your list, circle them twice in red.

Key words: ozone hole, greenhouse effect, environment, people, atmosphere, freons (chloroflurocarbons), chemicals, political effects, climate change, sea levels, fossil fuels, and political change.

Transcript for *Environmental Changes,* by Richard Somerville

1   My name is Richard Somerville and I'm going to talk to you about the

2   ozone hole and the greenhouse effect. Here are two examples of

3   change in the environment where people may be affecting natural

4   processes. We'll start with the ozone hole.

5   Ozone is a gas that occurs in small quantities naturally in the

6   atmosphere—mainly in the stratosphere, high above the surface. And

7   two scientists theorized in the 1970s that the ozone layer might be in

8 danger: that ozone in the stratosphere might gradually be depleted

9 because of the actions of man-made chemicals. The chemicals they

10 had in mind were freons (or chlorofluorocarbons), which are found in

11 refrigerators, air conditioners, and as solvents in the electronics

12 industry. And these scientists predicted a gradual decline over many

13 years if these chemicals continued to be produced.

14 What was actually found in the atmosphere, however, was a

15 dramatic surprise. In the early 1980s scientists in Antarctica,

16 measuring ozone levels from the ground, discovered that something

17 like half the ozone over the Antarctic continent was disappearing

18 every year during spring of the southern hemisphere, and then

19 replenishing itself later in the southern year. No one knew exactly

20 why this was happening, but the freons were suspects, and an

21 intensive research program was launched to see what was causing the

22 Antarctic ozone hole.

23 Scientists soon concluded that, indeed, freons (or

24 chlorofluorocarbons) were the culprits, and as a result the nations of

25 the world, in a remarkable series of political actions, signed treaties to

26 ban the manufacture of these chemicals. These were man-made

27 chemicals entirely; they don't occur in nature. They had been thought

28 to be inert and harmless environmentally, and so the ozone hole was a

29 surprise. But the result was a successful political action, and it's now

30 illegal to make these chemicals in the United States, and it will soon

31 be illegal everywhere. It's in a way a success story, one in which wise

32 public policy was undergirded by good scientific research. And the

33 result will benefit us all. We think that over a period of several

34 decades ozone levels will reach their natural amounts again and the

35 effects of the freons will have been undone.

36 By contrast, the greenhouse effect is not likely to have such a

37 clear-cut happy ending. The greenhouse effect is first of all a natural

38   phenomenon and a pervasive one. There are chemicals in the

39   atmosphere—including water vapor and carbon dioxide and methane

40   and others—which serve to trap heat that would otherwise escape

41   from the Earth into space and leave our planet much cooler. Without

42   our atmosphere and its natural greenhouse effect we'd have a harsh,

43   cold climate like that of the moon.

44   The worry is not that the greenhouse effect is there; we should be

45   grateful for it—it keeps our planet habitable. The concern is that we

46   people are changing it. There are now so many people on Earth

47   (nearly 6 billion, growing by almost 100 million per year), and these

48   people use so much energy, and generate most of it by burning coal

49   and oil and natural gas, which produce carbon dioxide when burned,

50   that people are becoming an influence on the global environment

51   rivaling that of natural processes. It's as though all the people on

52   Earth, having for millennia been spectators at the great natural

53   pageant of climate change, suddenly came up out of the audience

54   onto the stage and began to take a role in it themselves. It's never

55   happened before in human history.

56   Scientists disagree on how serious the threat to climate from an

57   enhanced greenhouse effect is. A consensus figure is that sometime in

58   the 21st century the planet will be noticeably warmer than it would

59   otherwise have been, perhaps 3 to 5° Fahrenheit warmer, and we'll

60   see other consequences as well. For example, sea level will rise. That's

61   happening for two reasons: one, when the ocean is warmer the warm

62   water takes up more volume than the cold water had, and second, as

63   the climate warms, ice on the land—in Greenland and Antarctica, on

64   continental glaciers—begins to melt and ends up in the sea. So in a

65   warm climate sea level is higher. In fact, we know from the geological

66   record that during the ice ages sea level was many meters lower than

67   it is today. So if the climate warms we'll see not only temperature

68   changes, but also sea level changes and we believe also alterations in

69   the natural pattern of storms and precipitation. It will all in all be

70   deleterious. There will surely be some winners from climate change—

71   cold countries may have longer growing seasons, for example—but

72   climate is something that we become used to, and the climate-

73   sensitive sectors of our economy like agriculture are adapted to

74   the present climate. So climate change is something to be

75   concerned about.

76   But altering human behavior to avert an enhanced greenhouse

77   effect will not be as easy as finding benign substitutes for freon. For

78   one thing, there are just too many people, and for another, they use

79   too much energy. And the most populous countries on earth (like

80   China and India) are rapidly industrializing, using coal and other

81   fossil fuels as their energy base. So it would require a remarkable

82   effort for the people of the world to first of all do the research to

83   understand climate, to monitor climate change, to figure out where

84   the greenhouse effect is most serious. And second, having understood

85   it to decide on and muster the political will to do something about it.

86   In a way, the struggle to repair the ozone hole is a kind of

87   paradigm—it's an example for us that shows that people can make a

88   difference and can come together to benefit the environment once

89   they've realized the seriousness of the problem, have come to a

90   scientific understanding of it, and then have found the political will to

91   do what needs to be done. I think the message from this is that we

92   are living in an age where people rival nature as a force for

93   environmental change and that scientific research is crucial in

94   understanding that change. Thank you.

Five-Step Follow-up

Step 1   **Observation**

Review your answers to the study questions and be sure you answered all parts.

Step 2   **Selection**

Select the blue circles from your answer to study question 5. These are ideas that you listed as main ideas, but were not in the transcript. Select the portions of the transcript that have double red circles. These are the main ideas that you did not detect until you read the transcript.

Step 3   **Analysis**

Analyze for accuracy. In group discussion, compare your answers to study question 1. What is the speaker's purpose in giving this speech? Through discussion, see if the group can arrive at consensus regarding the purpose of the speech and if it is stated or implied.

Using the responses to follow-up question 2, choose two ideas that you listed as main ideas that were not in the transcript. Choose two ideas that were main ideas in the transcript that did not appear in your list. Why did the main ideas not appear in your list?

____

____

____

____

Step 4   **Assessment**

If you had more than two places on the transcript that had double red circles it may mean that you are missing main points as you listen.

Step 5   **Action**

Develop a plan for action based on your analysis and assessment. Listen to the passage again and mentally note when the speaker states one of the important points and when he states supporting points. Make a mental outline of these points as a way to practice sorting and ranking ideas as you hear them.

EXERCISE 6.3

Welfare Reform
MARQUESSA BROWN

Directions

Student Workbook
page 208

This video selection is about ten minutes long. You need a red, blue, and black pen or pencil for this exercise.

Study Questions

1. What is the speaker's purpose in giving this speech? Is the purpose stated or implied? How do you know? Write your answer as a complete sentence.

   Her purpose is to share information about social welfare reform. The speaker clearly states her purpose, it is not implied.

2. What is the speech about? Write your answer as one complete sentence. Write as many key words as you can remember from this speech.

   The speech explains the history of social welfare reform in the United States from the 1930s to the present.

3. What do you think the speaker's schema or frame of reference is? How do you arrive at your decision about this?

   She appears very knowledgeable about her topic. She speaks without hesitation and is not using notes so one can assume she knows this topic well. This assumption leads one to infer that her schema for welfare reform is based on study of the topic and experience in explaining these ideas. In fact she is a professor of social work at Gallaudet University.

4. Listen to the selection again. While listening write the main points and list the supporting points below them.

◆ *Welfare programs began around 1935 with the New Deal and were designed to help middle- and lower-class people who had suffered economic loss as a result of the Depression.*

  • *The U.S. felt a need for welfare reform.*

◆ *Social Security was the first structured welfare program that included women and children.*

  • *This was the first time that we had retirement and disability programs.*

  • *The focus of welfare programs was on children.*

  • *Mothers could not get money for children if there was a man in the house.*

  • *Social workers were expected to raid homes to look for men and material goods.*

  • *The presence of a man or of material goods could be taken to mean that the woman did not need welfare support.*

◆ *Over time welfare programs grew rapidly and included whole families.*

  • *Women were allowed to have men in their homes.*

  • *Women or men could get welfare support if they were unemployed.*

  • *The U.S. economy declined and the number of families needing support increased.*

  • *Homelessness increased.*

◆ *An increasing amount of the national budget went toward welfare and more people complained about that, which led to welfare reform.*

     • *The total amount of the budget that goes toward welfare is really only 4%.*

     • *Public opinion holds that those who do not work should not get welfare support.*

◆ *Now states want to decrease the number of people on welfare and have a five-year welfare limit.*

     • *The Clinton administration began using block grants that allow states to have control over a portion of the funds.*

     • *The less states spend on welfare, the more money they have for other things.*

     • *States are trying to get people off welfare and back to work.*

◆ *Many women need training and help with child care in order to get off welfare.*

     • *Many women on welfare do not have job skills and need special training in how to dress and go to work.*

     • *Many on welfare cannot afford decent day care.*

____

____

____

____

____

5. Read the transcript. Circle key words in black. Look for main ideas and supporting ideas. Circle the main ideas in the transcript in red and underline the supporting ideas in red. Compare the transcript to the list you made in study question 4. Did you select the same main and supporting ideas when you listened to the tape the first and second time? If there are main ideas in your list that are not in the transcript, circle them in blue. If there are main ideas in the transcript that are not in your list, circle them twice in red.

Key words; social welfare reform, economic loss, women and children, money, Social Security, complaints, block grants, training, and day care.

Transcript for *Social Welfare Reform,* by Marquessa Brown

1   Hi. My name is Marquessa Brown. I'm going to share with you for a

2   coupla minutes some of my ideas about social welfare reform. Um, I

3   think I'll start with giving you a little bit of background about why

4   the United States has felt that we had a need for welfare reform. Um,

5   welfare as a program began in the United States around 1935 with the

6   New Deal. That was a period in our history immediately following the

7   Depression when many Americans had experienced economic loss.

8   Among those Americans that had experienced economic loss were

9   also some Americans who had been historically pretty middle class.

10   And the country felt that there was a need to help primarily middle

11   class people but also some poorer people who had experienced, um,

12   loss and deprivation following the Depression. Um, so again, around

13   1935 we had our first kinda structured um, social welfare program

14   in the United States. The primary program under the New Deal was

15   the Social Security program. And that was the first time that we had,

16   um, retirement for older people, and we eventually worked disability

17   into that program. We had our first welfare–child welfare programs.

18   And with the early child welfare programs the focus was primarily on

19   children, not the family in its entirety. So mothers were able to get

20   money for their children. Now the key was, moms could get money

21   for their children under the first, um, Social Security programs of—of

22   the—of 1935, but if there was a man in the house the mother could

23   not get money. So the program under Social Security was set up

24   primarily for mothers and children. Back in those days it was the—

25   the job of the social worker to make sure that mothers didn't have

26   men in their homes. So at that point, social workers could go into the

27   homes in the middle of the night and do their midnight raids and

28   make sure there was no man in the house. They would also check to

29   see what kind of material goods women had, because Social Security

30   wanted you to be poor. And if you had a nice radio, and if you had a

31   nice,um, electrical appliances then they didn't feel like you were poor

32   enough or, quote, deserving enough, and so they could take you off

33   of what was known as welfare. Later, around the forties, a case went

34   to the Supreme Court and the judgement was made that you could

35   not remove women from welfare because a male was in the

36   household. And that you basically had to do what was known as

37   simply a means test: to be sure that families met the, um, income

38   requirements; that their incomes were low enough to qualify for, um,

39   welfare under the Social Security program.

40   Over the years the Social Security—the—the—welfare programs

41   under Social Security changed somewhat. The amount of spending,

42   um, increased, um, women were allowed to—to have a male in the

43   household, provided either the female or the male were unemployed.

44   So we moved to a program that was called, um, child welfare/UN for

45   the unemployed. So there became more of a focus on the family. So

46   you wanted the male, the female, the mom, the dad, and the children

47   to all be supported under this welfare system. Anyway, the program

48   began to grow. One of the reasons I believe it grew was because as the

49   economy in the U.S. declined, the number of families requiring

50   welfare increased. So by the time Reagan became president and we

51   had high unemployment, then we began to have more families going

52   on welfare. And we also began to see more families becoming

53   homeless at that point. Well, as the program increased—as the

54   number of people on the program increased—Americans and the

55   Congress really became more concerned about the amounts of money

56   that were being spent on welfare. I think one of the things that we in

57   the U.S. never really recognized was even though it appeared that the

58   amount of money going into the welfare program (which is under the

59   Social Security Act) was increasing, it remained only 4% of the entire

60   U.S. budget. So the large percentage of money was never going into

61   the welfare program. But we as Americans began to complain more

62   and more about these lazy people who were getting a check, who

63   weren't doing anything, who were just having babies, and by golly, if

64   I'm workin' everybody's gotta work. So the more we complained and

65   the more the media told us that the numbers of people on welfare

66   was increasing and the U.S. budget was being—more of the money

67   was being spent on welfare, the more there was a public cry to do

68   something about this. So that's how we basically got to our welfare

69   reform. What has happened with the welfare reform under the

70   Clinton administration is, states are now permitted to make decisions

71   about how they want to spend their—their monies that are allotte—

72   their block—grants that are allotted under social security. The less

73   money that the states spend on supporting women and families on

74   welfare, the more money the states will get. So all of the states, um,

75   are trying to figure out ways to decrease the number of women and

76   the number of families on welfare. There's a lot of questioning about

77   how successful this program is going to be. But no woman is allowed

78   to stay on welfare for more than five years. There's a move in the

79   country to, um, train women to go into the workforce. That's been a

80   very complicated process because oftentimes, women have had long

81   histories of not working—do—and they don't have the clothes to go

82   to work. They are not structured in a way to understand about getting

83   up and going, um, they don't have a whole lot of understanding

84   about work behavior. So, the states have begun to set up training

85   programs to really teach women about work etiquette. Some of that's

86   been successful and some of it's not. The other issue has been day

87   care. Um, and if any people have been looking or, or listening to the

88   news, there's a lot in the papers and there's a lot in the media now

89   about day care. Because these women have had to find places or day

90   care centers to send their children. The problem has become we in

91   the U.S. don't provide affordable day care for people who are going to

92   be going to minimum wage jobs, um, and really can't afford day care.

93   Good day care probably costs more than $100 a week now. And that's

94   far more than many of these women are going to be earning when

95   they go to these low-paying kinds of jobs and go to these job training

96   programs. Um, so we've got two problems: women that aren't trained

97   and doing something to resolve the day care situation so that women

98   can go to work and feel safe about leaving their children in a day

99   care setting.

Five-Step Follow-up

Step 1　Observation

Review your answers to the study questions and be sure you answered all parts.

Step 2　Selection

Select the blue circles from your answer to study question 5. These are ideas that you listed as main ideas, but were not in the transcript. Select the portions of the transcript that have double red circles. These are the main ideas that you did not detect until you read the transcript.

Step 3　Analysis

Analyze for accuracy. In group discussion, compare your answers to study question 1. What is the speaker's purpose in giving this speech? Through discussion, see if the group can arrive at consensus regarding the purpose of the speech and if it is stated or implied.

Using the responses to follow-up question 2, choose two ideas that you listed as main ideas that are not in the transcript. Choose two main ideas in the transcript that did not appear in your list. Why did the main ideas not appear in your list?

____

____

____

____

Step 4　Assessment

If you had more than two places on the transcript that had double red circles it may mean that you are missing main points as you listen.

Step 5　Action

Develop a plan for action based on your analysis and assessment. Listen to the passage again and mentally note when the speaker states one of the important points and when she states supporting points. Make a mental outline of these points as a way to practice sorting and ranking ideas as you hear them.

Progress Tracking Sheet

This sheet is designed to help you keep track of which exercises you have completed and how well you have done on these exercises. See page 13 (Teacher's Guide page 20) for a full description of how to use the Progress Tracking Sheet.

Exercise Number	Date	First Performance	Study Questions	Follow-up Activity	Questions and Reminders	Date	Second Performance
Exercise 6.1 Quantitative							
Qualitative							
Exercise 6.2 Quantitative							
Qualitative							
Exercise 6.3 Quantitative							
Qualitative							
Quantitative Totals							

UNIT 7

Summarizing

Introduction

The ability to summarize or capture the gist of what is heard is one of the abilities central to the interpretation process. According to Tommola (1995), the process of summarizing is so important that it is often used as an aptitude test for candidates entering interpretation programs. Tommola writes "Among the various characteristics that interpreter aptitude tests attempt to measure, a central one is the ability to analyze the source message into its semantic elements, to create a representation of the content, and to retain this representation in memory so that it can be rendered in the target language" (p. 471). Tommola goes on to suggest that the ability to do macro processing or finding main ideas and awareness of the relationships between them demonstrate the absence of effortful processing, which is desirable for interpreters. "This process includes the restructuring of incoming information into more abstract units of meaning which subsume the lower-level details." Retrieval of the hierarchically stored abstract units is an essential aspect of consecutive and, to some extent, simultaneous interpreting. Another way to look at this is to think about the exercises in Unit 6 and see how the identification of main and supporting ideas can lead to strong summarization skills. The main ideas and supporting ideas when combined can yield a summary.

The Role of Summarizing in the Interpretation Process

As stated previously, summarization skills are often used as a part of the selection process for candidates entering an interpretation program. These skills are also an important part of the interpretation process itself, especially consecutive interpretation. The ability to recall the gist of the information presented leads to finding the rest of the relevant information in memory. An accurate and concise summary can "trigger" the memory of other related details. This kind of trigger may last only a short time, since interpreters generally are not trying to create long-term memories based on what they heard. Rather, they are relying heavily on working memory to process what they are hearing while they are interpreting.

There is a constant sorting of information during the interpretation process. The interpreter must determine which information is very important and which is less important. The interpreter makes this decision based their schema, what they know about the topic, and what they know about the audience. The interpreter also constantly sorts information into categories or topics.

While listening, it is generally apparent when the speaker has changed to a new topic. This topic shift must be represented in the interpretation. In some cases the interpreter may not know much about either the topic or the audience. The interpreter must then use prior knowledge and schemas of similar topics and audiences to determine what is important and what must not be deleted from the interpretation. For example, if the situation is a medical conference on the topic of diabetes, the interpreter may be able to assume that the audience has prior knowledge of this topic.

Analysis of the Target Audience

An analysis of the composition of the audience with which the interpreter is working is ordinarily studied in relation to the skill of simultaneous interpreting. It is studied here because this type of analysis takes time to develop and should be introduced as a critically important feature of any interpretation. Interpretation never occurs in isolation. Thus it is important to introduce the variable of audience analysis as early as feasible in the learning process. While the ability to provide a quick and accurate summary is a desirable skill for an interpreter to possess, there are many questions that must be considered before the summary is created. The target audience must be evaluated in terms of their composition and information needs. In addition to the actual content and arrangement of the linguistic information, cultural information must be considered. If the summary is created without regard to audience needs and cultural information, then the summary will not be as accurate as it could be.

There is more to creating a good summary, and later a good interpretation, than simply awareness of the ideas and their relationships. There is also the matter of cultural information that cannot be separated from the linguistic information. For example, if the speech is about Telecommunications Devices for the Deaf (TDD) usage, and the speech is being given to hearing people who may not have prior experience with the deaf community, the interpreter is obliged to analyze the audience prior to making the summary. It is important to know if the audience members have had any prior exposure to the deaf community and their telecommunications devices. The same sort of analysis process could be used if the topic were video production and the audience had no prior experience in that field. Sometimes it is not possible for the interpreter to know the composition of the audience and their prior collective knowledge. However, as an exercise, it is valuable to describe the audience so that you can use prediction skills and then determine the main points and whether they should be phrased with less or more detail.

Below is a list of factors that can affect audience composition. A selection from among these can create hypothetical audiences for you to "face." Based on the hypothetical audience composition, you can describe how you present the summarized information.

- Size:

  Large, over 50 people;

  Medium, 25 to 49 people;

  Small, under 25.

- Interview setting. 3 or 4 participants.
- Language used by the audience members and which register of that language is most appropriate for the setting and participants.
- Hearing status of the group members. This variable is important for signed language interpreters regardless of which type of signed language is used.

  All deaf members.

  All hearing members.

  Mix of hearing and deaf.

  Unknown, i.e., sometimes you do not know if there are any deaf people or any hearing people in the audience.

- Background knowledge of the group:

  Knowledgeable about a topic, e.g., a special conference on the topic and we assume those in attendance know the jargon and related background information.

To be sure, it will not always be possible for you to answer all the questions raised in this chapter before beginning a summary or an interpretation. There may be even more relevant variables than those mentioned here. Nevertheless you should be aware that there can be unanswered questions and, in that case, you can proceed to make decisions based on what can be observed plus what can be inferred from your observations. When working from that position, you must be ready to change to a different set of assumptions as information builds during the interpreting assignment. A good performance in a summarization exercise means you have considered all the decisions about the audience variables and text variables. Summary skills can also include presenting information in a paragraph or a single summary statement.

Summarization skills are valuable for the interpreter in training as well as for the working interpreter. A summary is the gist of the speech or talk. If you can quickly and accurately grasp the topic of the talk, then it will be easier to follow the speaker and the various lines of reasoning that the speaker might use. Summarization skills show that you can get the "big picture" of the speech and not get confused with the details and miss the point of the speech.

Discussion Questions

Discuss the following questions with your students to promote insight and increase awareness of the importance of developing summarization skills.

1. *How do summary skills in English relate to the interpretation process?*

   Creating a short summary may also be thought of as finding the gist of a passage. A summary can be a single sentence or a short paragraph. The ability to find the gist of a passage is often used as a predictor for interpretation skills. The presence of this ability shows that the interpreter is able to find the central organizing principle of the talk or text.

2. *Do you feel your summary of a text would be exactly the same as another person's summary?*

   Each person's summary may be slightly different in form but the meaning should be approximately the same. In other words, it should be possible for two people to agree on the most important points in a given text, even though they use different words to express the ideas.

3. *What happens when two people do not agree on what points are most important in a given passage or text?*

   First of all, the two people, if they are not interpreters, are not likely to realize that they do not see things the same way. If a conflict or misunderstanding arises, then it may become apparent that there is a difference in perception as to what is most important in what was said. It is possible that based on prior experiences, each person brings different perceptual information to each communicative event. Due to this difference in perceptual background information, two people might not agree on what is most important. For an interpreter, it is even more critical to be able to find the central organizing principles of a talk or text. The interpreter needs to be aware that there are various ways to see and understand things. When the interpreter can see several possible viewpoints, it is important for the interpreter to ask the speaker for clarification.

4. *What do you think will happen if the interpreter does not know how to create a succinct summary?*

    Ordinarily, the inability to make a quick and concise summary may not show up in everyday interpreting. However, the interpreter who can demonstrate a quick grasp of the material at hand is more likely to be able to render a faithful interpretation than an interpreter who is unable to sort out unimportant from important points.

Summarizing Exercises

Decide if you want to conduct these exercises in class, or if you want the students to do these exercises on their own time. If students do these exercises on their own, they must each have their own source tape. The exercises can be done in a group setting. Students respond by writing or drawing.

If you decide to conduct these exercises during class time, be sure all the students can see the TV monitor you are using. Check to see that the volume is appropriate for the number of students in the room. Ask the students to prepare themselves to listen carefully. Remind them not to write or draw while listening. Ask all students to refrain from making noise during the time the tape is being played.

Read the directions and explain them to the students. Allow time for questions after you have given the directions. You should plan at least five minutes to prepare the students for the exercise. Five minutes should be enough, if you have the group's attention, and if all equipment is ready and in working order. All tapes needed for these exercises must be cued to the correct spot. This includes the source tape and any tapes that will be used for recording.

EXERCISE 7.1

My First Teaching Experience
JANET PERKIN

Directions

Student Workbook
page 222

This selection is approximately two minutes long and should be followed by answering the study questions and then the follow-up. Find this selection on your tape. Adjust the volume as necessary. Begin by allowing yourself time to focus on the speaker's face. Listen to the selection. Do not write while listening. Do not read the transcript yet. Stop the tape at the end of this selection and answer the study questions. You will need three colored pens or pencils, red, blue, and black.

Study Questions

1. Turn on your recording device (audio or video). Describe the audience you envision listening to your summary. Use the audience analysis parameters in this chapter as a guide.

   Sample answer: This audience is a mix of both deaf and hearing people. There are about 15 people. They are there to meet a new person (Janet Perkin) in the neighborhood and she is giving a talk to let them get to know her a bit better.

2. Record a one-paragraph summary of this selection. The paragraph should contain four or five sentences and should be well organized. Do not write it down first. Transcribe it after you have recorded it.

   My first teaching job was in Durban, South Africa. I was the only English-speaking staff member. The Afrikaans-speaking teachers taught social studies. I taught math and scripture. The black teachers spoke Zulu and taught other subjects. So, the students had to be trilingual.

   I really enjoyed that unforgettable experience.

3. Record a one-sentence summary of this selection. Do not write it down
    first. Transcribe it after you have recorded it.

    My first teaching job was in South Africa in a mission school where the

    children were trilingual.

4. Listen to the selection again and answer study questions 2 and 3 again.
    Are your summaries different the second time? Do they differ in form
    only or in form and meaning?

    The summary should not contain phrases like "she said" or "the passage

    was about."

List the main points from both of your summary paragraphs in the space
provided. Circle in red any parts of your second summary that differ in
meaning from the first summary. Circle in blue any main points that are
listed in your second summary but not in the first.

Main Points Summary 1 (from question 2)

____

____

____

____

Main Points Summary 2 (from question 3)

____

____

____

____

____

____

____

____

5. Exchange the summary paragraph that you think is most accurate with a classmate or colleague and list the main points in that person's summary. Are these the same main points that you have selected?

    Differences can lead to class discussions regarding which information needs to be included in a good summary.

Transcript for *My First Teaching Experience,* by Janet Perkin

1   My name is Janet Perkin and I'm going to tell you about my first

2   teaching experience, which was at a mission school in South Africa. I

3   had been unable to get a job in the European schools over there, and

4   much to my delight and surprise I was accepted to teach at a black

5   mission school in—just outside Durban in South Africa.

6   The first day I had to go out there I drove in my car through the

7   sugarcane fields and eventually arrived at the white mission school

8   and found that I was the only English-speaking member of staff there.

9   Strangely enough, the other people were either Afrikaans-speaking

10 (which is a Dutch, uh, language) and then the other people—the

11 black teachers—all spoke Zulu. So it was rather strange that we were

12 all talking in three different languages, and the students had, uh,

13 lessons in these different languages. Social studies was taught in

14 Afrikaans, uh, math and scripture was taught in English, which was

15 my subjects, and, uh, Zulu was used in certain other subjects so they

16 had to be pretty good to be trilingual.

17   I really enjoyed my experience there; in fact, it's my favorite

18 teaching job and nothing could match it later on in life, because

19 education was so important to these people. I'll never ex—forget my

20 experience there.

Five-Step Follow-up

Step 1   Observation

Check your answers to be sure that you have answered all parts of all of the study questions.

Step 2   Selection

Refer to your answer to study question 4. Select the portions that are circled in red. These will be the portions of your second summary that differ in meaning from the first summary. Select the main ideas from your second summary that you circled in blue.

Work with students to see that they are not distracted by differences in form rather than meaning. You can refer back to Unit 6 and use the main point lists from the exercises in that unit. Those lists could also be made into good summaries. This additional practice may be helpful to students.

Step 3   **Analysis**

Study the portions of your work that you selected in step 2. Write down the reasons that the meaning differed in the second summary. Write down why the main ideas in your second list are more accurate than those in the first. Explain why your second list is different from the first. Read the transcript of the passage (not of your summaries) and compare your summaries to the speaker's words. If you find sections in the transcript of the passage that are important and do not show up in any of your summaries, circle them in black and create a new summary that includes this information.

____

____

____

____

____

Details and less important points do not belong in the summary paragraph. You can help students decide which points are least important and should not be in the summary.

Step 4   **Assessment**

In examining your work, see if your transcript includes phrases such as "this is about," "the man said," "I guess this was about," "and then the speaker said," or "I can't remember what came next." If you have phrases like this in your transcript, put a black line through them as they are not part of what the speaker said. The summary must contain the gist of what the speaker said and must not include any comments about the passage or about your performance in summarizing.

Comments about oneself or about the passage are called metacomments and are not part of the summary. Encourage students to summarize only the information in the passage, not their comments about the passage.

Step 5   **Action**

Continue practicing developing accurate, concise summaries. One suggestion is to select another passage from the accompanying video and follow the directions for summarizing. Answer the study questions and do the follow-up.

Refer students back to Unit 6 to work with the main point lists from those exercises. The main point lists can be adapted into summary paragraphs by using transitions and opening and closing sentences.

EXERCISE 7.2

Our Trip to Hong Kong
LESLIE RACH

Directions

Student Workbook
page 227

This selection is approximately four minutes long and should be followed by answering the study questions and then the follow-up. Find this selection on your tape. Adjust the volume as necessary. Begin by allowing yourself time to focus on the speaker's face. Listen to the selection. Do not write while listening. Do not read the transcript yet. Stop the tape at the end of this selection and answer the study questions. You will need three colored pens or pencils, red, blue, and black.

Study Questions

1. Turn on your recording device (audio or video). Describe the audience for which your summary is intended. Use the audience analysis parameters in this unit as a guide.

    The audience consists of three deaf women who want to know about Leslie's trip to Hong Kong.

2. Record a one-paragraph summary of this selection. The paragraph should contain four or five sentences and should be well organized. Do not write it down first. Transcribe it after you have recorded it.

    My husband and I took a trip to Hong Kong. We flew from North Carolina

    toward Alaska but the pilot turned the plane around due to mechanical

    problems. We landed in Anchorage with ambulances lining the runway.

Later we saw that one engine was on fire, but we had not known that. We

stayed in Anchorage one night and flew to Hong Kong the next day.

3. Record a one-sentence summary of this selection. Do not write it down first. Transcribe it after you have recorded it.

When my husband and I were traveling to Hong Kong, we had an

unscheduled emergency landing in Alaska due to an engine that caught

on fire.

4. Listen to the selection again and answer study questions 2 and 3 again. Are your summaries different the second time? Do they differ in form only or in form and meaning?

____

____

____

____

____

____

____

List the main points from both of your summary paragraphs in the space provided. Circle in red any parts of your second summary that differ in meaning from the first summary. Circle in blue any main points that are listed in your second summary but not in the first.

Main Points Summary 1 (from question 2)

____

____

____

____

____

____

____

____

Main Points Summary 2 (from question 3)

____

____

____

____

____

____

____

____

5. Exchange the summary paragraph that you think is most accurate with a classmate or colleague and list the main points in that person's summary. Are these the same main points that you selected?

   Differences can lead to class discussions regarding which information needs to be included in a good summary.

Transcript for *Our Trip to Hong Kong,* by Leslie Rach

1 Hi, I'm Leslie Rach and I'm gonna tell a story about a trip I took to

2 Hong Kong four years ago, in the winter. My husband and I were

3 supposed to go from Dulles airport to North Carolina, where we

4 would then fly to Tokyo, Japan, and connect on a flight to Hong

5 Kong.

6   As it turned out we did go to North Carolina and then we spent

7 about five hours in the air and everything was going fine until the

8 pilot made an announcement in Japanese, of course, because we were

9 on Japan airlines. And I should go back and add that when we were

10 on the tarmac in North Carolina, the flight attendants were standing,

11 um, out by the where the plane was going to take off and they were

12 waving very formally to wave us goodbye on our way off to Japan. So

13 that was an indication of what was to come.

14   We, uh, were about one hour outside of Anchorage, Alaska, to the

15 west of Anchorage, and the pilot made an announcement, uh, that we

16 would be turning around because of mechanical difficulties and didn't

17 elaborate on that really at all. And everyone seemed unusually calm

18 on the plane. I couldn't believe it. I thought someone should be

19 screaming, although I wasn't screaming, someone should have been.

20 So anyway, he turned the plane around and we ended up landing in a

21 cargo airport in Anchorage, which indicated that it was pretty serious,

22 although none of us really knew it at the time. But as we were

23 landing, on the runway, on either side of where we were landing,

24   there were about 100 ambulances and fire engines lined up all along

25   the runway. And, um, so then we started to get the feeling that it was

26   pretty serious. And we ended up landing and we got off of the plane

27   and went into the airport and through the window we could see that

28   one of the engines, the right engine, was on fire.

29   And of course none of us had known this the whole time. And

30   several of the passengers immediately got out their cameras and out

31   of the window they started snapping pictures of the burning fuselage.

32   So, um, it was quite an adventure and we spent the night in an

33   airport in Anchorage, I mean in a hotel in Anchorage that evening.

34   And my husband and I, like I said, thought we were going to Hong

35   Kong, but it was December, and so we were dressed very summer

36   like. I had on a thin wool jacket and very thin summer pants. But we

37   were determined to see some of downtown Anchorage since we were

38   sure it was the only time we would be there in our whole lives. So we

39   did make a little go of the city and there was only about maybe about

40   three hours of daylight even thought it was the middle of the day.

41   And it was very gloomy daylight, I should add.

42   And the next morning we were to get back on a plane and head

43   for Hong Kong as originally scheduled. And they put us back on the

44   same plane. It was very perplexing. But it turned out they had

45   replaced the engine overnight with another engine that had been

46   flown in from Tokyo. So we all got back on the plane with much

47   trepidation and flew to Hong Kong without event and landed the

48   next day.

49   So that's the story of my trip, the only trip I took to Asia and I'm

50   supposed to go this winter again. So, I have some reservations, but

51   will be brave.

Five-Step Follow-up

Step 1   Observation

Check your answers to be sure that you answered all parts of all of the study questions.

Step 2   Selection

Refer to your answer to study question 4. Select the portions that are circled in red. These are the portions of your second summary that differ in meaning from the first summary. Select the main ideas from your second summary that you circled in blue.

Step 3   Analysis

Study the portions of your work that you selected in step 2. Write down the reasons that the meaning differed in the second summary. Write down why the main ideas in your second list are more accurate than those in the first. Explain why your second list is different from the first. Read the transcript of the passage (not of your summaries) and compare your summaries to the speaker's words. If you find sections in the transcript of the passage that are important and do not show up in any of your summaries, circle them in black and create a new summary that includes this information.

____

____

____

____

____

Step 4   Assessment

In examining your work, see if your transcript includes phrases such as "this is about," "the man said," "I guess this was about," "and then the speaker said," or "I can't remember what came next." If you have phrases like this in your transcript, put a black line through them, as they are not part of what the speaker said. The summary must contain the gist of what the speaker said and must not include any comments about the passage or about your performance in summarizing.

Step 5   Action

Continue practicing developing accurate, concise summaries. One suggestion is to select another passage from the accompanying video and follow the directions for summarizing. Answer the study questions and do the follow-up.

EXERCISE 7.3

The Criminal Justice System
EUGENE CORBETT

Directions

Student Workbook
page 233

This selection is approximately five minutes long and should be followed by the study questions and the follow-up. Find this selection on your tape. Adjust the volume as necessary. Begin by allowing yourself time to focus on the speaker's face. Listen to the selection. Do not write while listening. Do not read the transcript yet. Stop the tape at the end of this selection and answer the study questions. You will need three colored pens or pencils, red, blue, and black.

Study Questions

1. Turn on your recording device (audio or video). Describe the audience you envision listening to your summary is intended. Use the audience analysis parameters in this chapter as a guide.

   I envision the audience as all deaf, about 40 people, some of whom use ASL and some a mixture of ASL and English-based signing. It is a lecture setting.

2. Record a one-paragraph summary of this selection. The paragraph should contain for or five sentences and should be well organized, presenting the information in the same order in which it was originally presented. Do not write it down first. Transcribe it after you record it.

   The criminal justice system has four main parts. The first part is the arrest,

   which happens when a person is suspected of committing a crime. The

   second is prosecution, which happens in a courtroom appearance and is a

   preliminary hearing. Next is the arraignment, during which the defendant

> *pleads guilty or not guilty. The fourth phase is corrections, which means*

> *the person may be incarcerated or put on probation.*

3. Record a one-sentence summary of this selection. Do not write it down first. Transcribe it after you have recorded it.

> *The four parts of the criminal justice system begin with the arrest phase and*

> *end with the corrections phase.*

4. Listen to the selection again and answer study questions 2 and 3 again. Are your summaries different the second time? Do they differ in form only or in form and meaning?

____

____

____

____

____

____

____

List the main points from both of your summary paragraphs in the space provided. Circle in red any parts of your second summary that differ in meaning from the first summary. Circle in blue any main points that are listed in your second summary but not in the first.

Main Points Summary 1 (from question 2)

____

____

____

____

____

____

____

____

Main Points Summary 2 (from question 3)

____

____

____

____

____

____

____

____

5. Exchange the summary paragraph that you think is most accurate with a classmate or colleague and list the main points in that person's summary. Are these the same main points that you selected?

   Differences can lead to class discussions regarding which information needs to be included in a good summary. The main points should be included in the same order in which they occurred in the original text.

Transcript for *The U.S. Criminal Justice System,* by Eugene Corbett

1   Today I'd like to give you an overview of the criminal justice system

2   in America. The systems running throughout the country are

3   somewhat different but all achieve the same purpose. There are

4   basically four parts of the criminal justice system: the arrest phase, the

5   prosecution phase, the arraignment phase in court, and the

6   correctional aspect. These components all to—go together to make up

7   the criminal justice system. They—as I said earlier—they vary

8   depending on the county, the state, and also the federal level. As you

9   know, there are various arresting agencies in this country: the FBI, the

10   Secret Service, as well as the metropolitan police department.

11   Let's start with phase one. A person—when a person is arrested,

12   there's probable cause to believe that he or she has committed a

13   crime. At that point, the police officer will escort the individual under

14   arrest for processing. There are several things that happen during the

15   processing stage. The person is booked, as they say sometimes. And

16   during that process the police officer will run a criminal record check

17   to see whether the person has any other charges or is wanted by other

18   state or county officials. He or she is also fingerprinted and that

19   information is sent to the FBI.

20   Subsequently to that, the individual is brought before the court.

21   That is called the initial appearance. At that time the prosecutor will

22   determine whether or not there is probable cause to believe that this

23   individual has committed an offense. There is also the point that if

24   there's no probable cause to believe the person can be released, and

25   this is called "no paper." The case is then "no-papered." If the

26   prosecutor feels that the individual has committed offense, he will

27   hold the case for what is called a preliminary hearing. At this point

28   the defendant appears before the court for what is called, again, the

29   preliminary hearing. It is at that time the prosecutor will present

30   evidence before the judge as to the defendant's conduct in the

31   community, for that particular crime. If the court finds probable cause

32   at that point, the individual will be detained for an arraignment. It is

33   also during that time that the charges can be lessened from, for

34   example, assault to simple assault. And also the defendant may be

35   able to play—play—plead guilty to a lesser included offense such as

36   simple assault. If not, the case continues to the arraignment part.

37   The arraignment part will consider the defendant appearing

38   before the court, at which time he or she will plead guilty or not

39   guilty to the formal charges presented by the prosecutor. The formal

40   charges are made up of two forms: one is called an indictment, the

41   other called an information. The information is the formal charges,

42   written charges by the prosecutor. The indictment is handed down

43   from the grand jury. At this time, the defendant, if he pleads guilty to

44   the offense is—a trial date is set. During trial, if the defendant is

45   found guilty he is then sent to the probation office on preparation for

46   a presentence report, and sentencing is set. At that time, the

47   defendant is found—is sentenced and he's incarcerated at the criminal

48   justice system part. He will remain in custody of the department of

49   corrections or whatever correctional facility for the time he is

50   sentenced and released on parole.

Five-Step Follow-up

Step 1   Observation

Check your answers to be sure that you answered all parts of all of the study questions.

Step 2   Selection

Refer to your answer to study question 4. Select the portions that are circled in red. These will be the portions of your second summary that differ in meaning from the first summary. Select the main ideas from your second summary that you circled in blue.

Step 3   Analysis

Study the portions of your work that you selected in step 2. Write down the reasons that the meaning differed in the second summary. Write down why the main ideas in your second list are more accurate than those in the first. Explain why your second list is different from the first. Read the transcript of the passage (not of your summaries) and compare your summaries to the speaker's words. If you find sections in the transcript of the passage that are important and do not show up in any of your summaries, circle them in black and create a new summary that includes this information.

____

____

____

____

____

____

Step 4   Assessment

In examining your work, see if your transcript includes phrases such as "this is about," "the man said," "I guess this was about," "and then the speaker said," or "I can't remember what came next." If you have phrases like this in your transcript, put a black line through them as they are not part of what the speaker said. The summary must contain the gist of what the speaker said and must not include any comments about the passage or about your performance in summarizing.

Step 5   Action

Continue practicing developing accurate, concise summaries. One suggestion is to select another passage from the accompanying video and follow the directions for summarizing. Answer the study questions and do the follow-up.

Progress Tracking Sheet

This sheet is designed to help you keep track of which exercises you have completed and how well you have done on these exercises. See page 13 (Teacher's Guide page 20) for a full description of how to use the Progress Tracking Sheet.

Exercise Number	Date	First Performance	Study Questions	Follow-up Activity	Questions and Reminders	Date	Second Performance
Exercise 7.1 Quantitative							
Qualitative							
Exercise 7.2 Quantitative							
Qualitative							
Exercise 7.3 Quantitative							
Qualitative							
Quantitative Totals							

References

The American Heritage Dictionary of the English Language, 3rd Edition (1992). Houghton-Mifflin.

Anderson, G., & Stauffer, L. (1990). *Identifying standards for the training of interpreters for deaf people.* University of Arkansas. Rehabilitation Research and Training Center on Deafness and Hearing Impairment.

Atkinson, R.C., & Shiffrin, R.M. (1968). Human memory: A proposed system and its control processes. In K.W. Spence (Ed.), *The Psychology of learning and motivation: Advances in research and theory.* New York: Academic Press.

Baddeley, A. (1990). *Human memory: Theory and practice.* Hillsdale, NJ: Erlbaum.

Baker, M., (1992). *In other words: A coursebook on translation.* New York: Routledge.

Bowen, D., & Bowen, M. (1989). Aptitude for interpreting. In L. Gran & J. Dodds (Eds.), *The theoretical and practical aspects of teaching conference interpretation* (pp. 109–127). Trieste, Italy: Campanotto Editore, Udine.

Bruner, J. S. (1966). *The process of education.* Cambridge, MA: Harvard University Press.

Cokely, D. (1986). The effects of time lag on interpreter errors. *Sign Language Studies.* 53. 341–376.

Cokely, D. (1992a). The effect of lag time on interpreter errors. In D. Cokely (Ed.), *Sign language interpreters and interpreting* (pp.39–69). Silver Spring, MD: Linstok Press.

Cokely, D. (1992b). *Interpretation:A sociolinguistic model.* Silver Spring, MD: Linstok Press.

Conference of Interpreter Trainers (1998). *CIT position paper: Instructional class size in interpreter training,* 18 (3), p.21.

Dancette, J. (1997). Mapping meaning and comprehension in translation. In J. Danks, et al. (Eds.), *Cognitive processes in translation and interpreting* (pp. 77–104). Thousand Oaks, CA: Sage Publications.

Danks, J. et al. (Eds.) (1997). *Cognitive processes in translation and interpreting.* Thousand Oaks, CA: Sage Publications.

Daro, V., & Fabbro, F. (1994). Verbal memory during simultaneous interpretation: Effects of phonological interference. *Applied Linguistics, 15,* 365–381.

DeGroot, A. (1997). The cognitive study of translation and interpretation. In J. Danks, et al. (Eds.), *Cognitive processes in translation and interpreting* (pp.25–57). Thousand Oaks, CA: Sage Publications.

Fleetwood, E. (1998). Personal communication.

Funk and Wagnall's Standard Dictionary (1983). New York: Harper Collins.

Gerver, D. (1976). Empirical studies of simultaneous interpretation: A review and a model. In R.W. Brislin (Ed.), *Translation: Applications and research* (pp. 165–207). New York: Gardner.

Gile, D. (1995). *Basic concepts and models for interpreter and translator training.* Philadelphia: John Benjamins.

Gile, D. (1997). Conference interpreting as a cognitive management problem. In J. Danks, et al. (Eds.), *Cognitive processes in translation and interpreting* (pp.196–215). Thousand Oaks, CA: Sage Publications.

Gonzalez, R. et al. (1991). *Fundamentals in court interpretation: Theory, policy and practice.* Durham, NC: Carolina Academic Press.

Ingram, R., (1984). Teaching declage skills. In M. L. McIntire (Ed.), *New dialogues in interpreter education: Proceedings of the Fourth National Conference of Interpreter Trainers Convention* (pp. 291–308). Silver Spring: MD.

Johnson, R.E., Patrie, C., & Roy, C. (1988). *Master of Arts in Interpretation Curriculum* Washington, DC: Gallaudet University.

Kalina, S. (1992). Discourse processing and interpreting strategies-An approach to the teaching of interpreting. In C. Dollerup & A. Loddegaard (Eds.), *Teaching translation and interpreting training, talent and experience* (pp. 251–258). Philadelphia: John Benjamins.

Kelly, L. (1979). *The true interpreter: A history of translation theory and practice in the west.* New York: St. Martin's Press.

Kitano, H. (1993). La traduction de la langue parlee. In A. Clas & P. Bouillon (Eds.), *La traductiuqe: Etudes et recherches de traduction par ordinateur* (pp. 408–422). Montreal: Les Presses de l'Universite de Montreal.

Kurz, I. (1992). Shadowing exercises in interpreter training. In C. Dollerup & A. Loddegaard (Eds.), *Teaching translation and interpreting training, talent and experience* (pp. 245–250). Philadelphia: John Benjamins.

Lambert, S. (1992). Aptitude testing for simultaneous interpretation at the University of Ottawa. In L. Gran & J. Dodds (Eds.), *The interpreter's newsletter.* Trieste: University of Trieste Press.

Lambert, S. (1989). Plenary session. In S. Wilcox (Ed.), *New dimensions in interpreter education: Evaluation and critique* (pp. 113–125). Conference of Interpreter Trainers.

Lambert, S. (1988). A human information processing and cognitive approach to the training of simultaneous interpreters. In D. L. Hammond (Ed.), *Language at crossroads: Proceedings of the 29th Annual Conference of the American Translators Association* (pp. 379-387). Medford, NJ: Learned Information.

Larson, M. (1984). *Meaning based translation: A guide to cross-language equivalence.* Lanham, MD: University of America Press.

Longley, P. (1989). The use of aptitude testing in the selection of students for conference interpretation training. In L. Gran & J. Dodds (Eds.), *The theoretical and practical aspects of teaching conference interpretation* (pp. 105–109). Campanotto Editore, Udine.

MacWhinney (1997). Simultaneous interpretation and the competition model. In J. Danks, et al. (Eds.), *Cognitive processes in translation and interpreting* (pp. 215–233). Thousand Oaks, CA: Sage Publications.

Malakoff, M., & Hakuta, K. (1991). Translation skill and metalinguistic awareness in bilinguals. In E. Bialystok (Ed.), *Language processing and language awareness in bilingual children.* (pp. 141–166). New York: Oxford University Press.

Moser, B. (1997). Beyond curiosity: Can interpreting research meet the challenge? In J. Danks, et al. (Eds.), *Cognitive processes in translation and interpreting* (pp. 176-195). Thousand Oaks, CA: Sage Publications.

Moser–Mercer (1983). Defining aptitude for simultaneous interpretation. In M. L. McIntire (Ed.), *New dialogues in interpreter education: Proceedings of the Fourth National Conference of Interpreter Trainers Convention* (pp. 43–70). Silver Spring, MD: RID Publications.

Oller, J. (1988). Making sense in interpreter education programs: Evaluation. In S. Wilcox (Ed.), *New dimensions in interpreter education: Evaluation and critique. Proceedings of the Seventh National Convention of the Conference of Interpreter Trainers.* (pp. 1–20). Conference of Interpreter Trainers.

Paradis, M. (1994). Toward a neurolinguistic theory of simultanoues translation: The framework. *International Journal of Psycholinguistics,* 10, 319–355.

Patrie, C. (1994). *The readiness to work gap.* Conference of Interpreter Trainers.

Roberts, R. (1987). Spoken language interpreting vs. sign language interpreting. In K. Kummer (Ed.), *Proceedings of the 28th Annual Conference of the American Translators Association* (pp. 293–307). Albuquerque, NM: Learned Information Inc.

Roberts, R. (1992). Student competencies: Defining, teaching, and evaluating. In E.A. Winston (Ed.), *Student competencies: Defining, teaching, and evaluating* (pp. 1–18). Conference of Interpreter Trainers.

Schweda Nicholson, N. (1988). Interpreter evaluation: The whole does not always equal the sum of its parts. In S. Wilcox (Ed.), *New dimensions in interpreter education: Evaluation and critique* (pp. 65–68). Conference of Interpreter Trainers.

Schweda Nicholson, N. (1996). Perspectives on the role of memory in interpretation: A critical review of recent literature. In M. Jerome-O'Keefe (Ed.), *Global Vision: Proceedings of the 37th Annual Conference of the American Translators Association* (pp. 99–113). Alexandria, VA: The American Translator's Association.

Seal, B. (1999) Educational interpreters document efforts to improve. *VIEWS,* 16(2), p. 14. Silver Spring, MD: Registry of Interpreters for the Deaf.

Seleskovitch, D., & Lederer, M. (1989). *A systematic approach to teaching interpretation.* Silver Spring, MD: Registry of Interpreters for the Deaf.

Shreve, G., & Koby, G. (1997). Introduction: What's in the black box? Cognitive science and translation studies. In J. Danks, et al. (Eds.), *Cognitive processes in translation and interpreting* (pp. xi–xviii). Thousand Oaks, CA: Sage Publications.

Sunnari, M. (1995). Processing strategies in simultaneous interpreting: Experts vs. novices. In C. Nixon (Ed.), *Connections: Proceedings of the 36th Annual Conference of the American Translators Association* (pp. 157–165). Alexandria, VA: American Translator's Association.

Taylor, C. (1989). Textual memory and the teaching of consecutive interpretation. In L. Gran & J. Dodds (Eds.), *The Theoretical and practical aspects of teaching conference interpretation* (pp. 177–185). Campanotto Editore, Udine.

Tulvig, E. (1983). *Elements of episodic memory.* Oxford: Oxford University Press.

Waubonsee Community College (1993). *Interpreter training programs in the U.S. and Canada.* Sugar Grove, IL: Waubonsee Community College Press.

Ur, P. (1991). *Teaching listening comprehension.* Cambridge, UK: Cambridge University Press.

We hope you enjoyed
English Skills Development
by Carol Patrie...

If you would like to learn more about DawnSignPress products, please complete the following information and send it to us. We will send you a free catalog and a $10 coupon good toward the purchase of any DawnSignPress published material (not valid with distributed titles).

Name ____

Mailing (home) Address ________________________________

City ___________________State_______Zip____________

Country ____

Home Phone (_____)______________E-mail:______________

Program/School/Place where you teach__________________

____

Department ____

Mailing (work) Address ________________________________

City ___________________State_______Zip____________

Country ____

Work Phone (_____)______________E-mail:______________

Where did you purchase this installment of *The Effective Interpreting Series?*

____

____

6130 Nancy Ridge Drive, San Diego, CA 92121
V/TTY: 858-625-0600   FAX: 858-625-2336
TOLL FREE: 1-800-549-5350 / VISIT US AT www.dawnsign.com

WFL183